Developing Successful Social Media
Plans in Sport Organizations

Titles in the Sport Management Library

— • —

Case Studies in Sport Marketing

— • —

Developing Successful Social Media Plans in Sport Organizations

— • —

Developing Successful Sport Marketing Plans, 4th Edition

— • —

Developing Successful Sport Sponsorship Plans, 4th Edition

— • —

Economics of Sport, 2nd Edition

— • —

Foundations of Sport Management, 3rd Edition

— • —

Fundamentals of Sport Marketing, 4th Edition

— • —

Law in Sport: Concepts and Cases, 4th Edition

— • —

Media Relations in Sport, 3rd Edition

— • —

Sponsorship for Sport Managers

— • —

Sport Facility Management:
Organizing Events and Mitigating Risks, 2nd Edition

— • —

Sport Governance in the Global Community

— • —

Ticket Operations and Sales Management in Sport

— • —

For an updated list of Sport Management Library titles please visit:

www.fitpublishing.com/FiTCategorySportManagementLibrary.html

Developing Successful Social Media Plans in Sport Organizations

Jimmy Sanderson, PhD
Clemson University

Christopher Yandle, MS
Georgia Institute of Technology

AUTHORS

FiT Publishing
A Division of the International Center for Performance Excellence
375 Birch Street, WVU-CPASS, PO Box 6116
Morgantown, WV 26506-6116
www.fitpublishing.com

Library of Congress Card Catalog Number: 2015933052

ISBN: 978-1-935412-97-7

Cover Design: Bellephron Productions

Cover Photos: © Pressureua | Dreamstime.com—Social Media Signs Photo; Background art: © Bantuquka | Dreamstime.com

Production Editor: Nita Shippy

Copyeditor: Danielle Costello

Typesetter: Bellerophon Productions

Proofreader: Matt Brann

Indexer: Matt Brann

Printed by: Publisher's Graphics

10 9 8 7 6 5 4 3 2 1

FiT Publishing
A Division of the International Center for Performance Excellence
West Virginia University
375 Birch Street, WVU-CPASS
PO Box 6116
Morgantown, WV 26506-6116
800.477.4348 (toll free)
304.293.6888 (phone)
304.293.6658 (fax)
Email: fitcustomerservice@mail.wvu.edu
Website: www.fitpublishing.com

Contents

Acknowledgments

It is my sincere hope that this book will serve as a role model for how fruitful collaborations between academic researchers and industry practitioners can be in sport. I want to express my sincere thanks to Matt Brann with FiT for his vision in conceptualizing this book and his foresight to conceive it as a partnership between people in these two fields. When Matt asked me whom I would want to partner with in sport, Chris Yandle was the first name that came to mind. The things Chris does in social media continually impress me, and he inspires me to set no limits on what can be achieved.

I am also thankful for the many wonderful people who work in sport and social media who have been so willing to have conversations about this fascinating topic. I want to acknowledge especially Jeff Kallin and Jonathan Gantt with Clemson Athletics along with Lucas McKay, the Director of Operations for Men's Basketball at Clemson University, for always being willing to talk social media and share their experiences.

—Jimmy Sanderson

If any of you have followed me on Twitter or social media, then you know how much I love to tweet and how enamored I am by what people post, when they post, and why they post. The wonderful thing about social media: It's the world's greatest classroom. We are all still learning something new every day. That is why I eagerly jumped at the opportunity to be a part of this book.

Thank you to Jimmy Sanderson for his friendship and for providing me with an opportunity to continue the academic side of my career. Thank you to the University of Miami and Georgia Tech Athletic Administration for supporting me in pursuit of continual education and teaching. Thank you to my good friend Kevin DeShazo, who reached out to me four years ago when I was at Baylor because he saw something in me. His friendship—both personal and professional—has been a driving force for me as a student of social media.

—Chris Yandle

Foreword

Social media and sports. That's not a hot-button topic at all, is it? If you spend any time at all on Twitter (and since you're reading this book, I'm guessing you do) you know that sports and social media go together like peanut butter and jelly. Also, oil and water. It is one big, messy, loud, crazy place of scores and infographics, GIFs and #hottakes, banter and emotion.

And I love it. So much so that I've made a career out of working with sports organizations as it relates to social media. Which is why I also love this book that Jimmy Sanderson and Chris Yandle—two of the best in their respective fields (#SportsBiz, as we say on The Twitter)—have put together. They look at social media for sports organizations (college and pro) from every angle. At this point, we get the why of social media. Or at least I hope we do. Not enough, though, is written about the how. At least not by those who are actually doing the work on a daily basis. These guys live and breathe this world every day.

What Jimmy and Chris have done is lay out the how. From marketing to communications, coaches to players, compliance to ticket sales, fundraising and more, social media isn't as easy as crafting a funny tweet and hoping it goes viral. It takes a significant amount of planning and coordination, of goal-setting and measuring, of listening and responding, modifying and praying. Then rinse and repeat.

Through interviews with the best social media pros in the athletics space, they get down to the nitty gritty of not only what social media means to a sports organization, but how to put a successful plan in place—and in terms that anyone in the organization can understand. Though they still haven't settled the debate on whether GIF is pronounced with a hard or soft g.

This isn't another book you read and think, "Oh, that was nice," only to put it on the shelf (or your Kindle archive) to never be seen again. The ideas, practices, and questions in this book are things I have used with clients in the athletics space. It is a blueprint for success, or at the very least to put you on the path to success.

If you work in the world of social media and sports, or one day hope to join this beautifully chaotic industry, this book will be an invaluable resource for you. Keep it on your desk or in your messenger bag (we don't use briefcases anymore, do we?). Use it as a guide for your organization. Reference it often. And by all means, tweet out your favorite pieces of wisdom (as well as kind words to the authors for providing you with such awe).

Kevin DeShazo
Founder of Fieldhouse Media
Author of *iAthlete: Impacting Student-Atheltes of a Digital Generation*

1

Why Sport Organizations Need a Social Media Plan

INTRODUCTION

In the span of the last decade, social media technologies have proliferated across society. These platforms have become so entrenched in many people's everyday lives that it seems difficult to fathom that just a little over 10 years ago, Facebook, Twitter, Pinterest, YouTube, Google+, and Snapchat did not exist. Although usage of these platforms is changing constantly, estimates of the audiences using social media are staggering. For example, Facebook reports 1.35 billion monthly active users as of September 30, 2014 (Facebook, 2014). At the time of this writing (January, 2015), the current population of the Earth is approximately 7.125 billion people, which means that approximately one out of every five people on the planet has a Facebook account! While Facebook leads the pack, other platforms nonetheless have impressive user bases. These include the following:

Table 1.1	
Google+	540 million users (Smith, 2015)
LinkedIn	300 million users (LinkedIn's Newsroom, n.d.)
Twitter	288 million monthly active users (About Twitter, n.d.)
Instagram	300 million users (300 million, 2014)
Pinterest	53 million monthly active users (Bercovici, 2014)

Then take into account platforms like Snapchat, which is estimated to have more than 100 million monthly active users (MacMillan & Rusli, 2014), and Tumblr, which reports 217.8 million blogs that contain 100.3 billion posts (Tumblr, n.d.), and it is not difficult to see how much social media platforms have taken hold across the world.

While social media has changed many sectors of business and society, its effect on the sport industry is among the most significant examples of its impact (Sanderson, 2011a; Sanderson & Kassing, 2014). Consider that on any given day, sport reporters are tweeting

information about news that they are "hearing" about a potential coaching change or player transaction, an athlete posts a photo of some aspect of daily life on Instagram, and a team posts pictures on Facebook to encourage fans to attend an upcoming game. There are, of course, a multitude of other outcomes that occur at the intersection of social media and sport, and the sheer amount of data posted daily on social media sites can easily become overwhelming. Accordingly, it is imperative for sport organizations to have a plan, or a vision, for how social media will work for them. Social media is a powerful tool that should be prioritized, not treated as a task that can be outsourced to interns or, at worst, simply ignored.

A social media plan includes steps for how social media will be employed to further organizational goals, as well as how social media use by athletes and other organizational employees will be managed. Although employees' social media use is of concern for any organization, given the high visibility of athletes and coaches, it is imperative that social media use by these individuals is incorporated into a sport organization's social media plan. It is easy to say "we need a social media plan," but what exactly does that mean? This text serves as a resource for personnel in sport organizations charged with managing social media to answer that question. To begin, it is important to understand what is meant by the term "social media" and why social media has become such a major part of the sport industry.

SOCIAL MEDIA DEFINED

Social media is "architected by design to readily support participation, peer-to-peer conversation, collaboration and community" (Meraz, 2009, p. 682) and is characterized by

> activities, practices, and behaviors among communities of people who gather online to share information, knowledge, and opinions using conversational media . . . Web-based applications that make it possible to create and easily transmit content in the form of words, pictures, videos, and audios. (Safko & Brake, 2009, p. 6)

Social media, then, is about *creating*, *sharing*, and *having conversations*. This is where sport enters the equation. There are few topics (perhaps politics and religion) that can spark a conversation like sport can, and sport is a commonality that can unite (and at times, divide) people from all walks of life. It is not uncommon for people to talk about

sport at the office, at family gatherings, at the local bar, or via sport-talk radio. While these conversations still certainly occur, social media now provides a platform for these discussions to take place at the convenience of the user, enables these discussions to transcend boundaries of space and time, and allows users to self-publish without needing a gatekeeper for access.

As a result, social media use by sport organizations, athletes, and sport journalists has escalated, and it is not uncommon for sport to prompt heavy traffic on social media. For instance, during Super Bowl XLIX, Twitter reported that 28.4 million tweets were sent about the game (Gibbs, 2015). This activity prompted one journalist to note that Twitter has been established as "a Super Bowl party within a party, where people expect to share, and be entertained, during big live events" (Gross, 2014, para. 9). Additionally, during the inaugural College Football playoff games on January 1, 2015, there were 2.56 million tweets sent about the University of Oregon vs. Florida State University matchup in the Rose Bowl, while the Sugar Bowl contest between the University of Alabama and Ohio State University generated just over 1.9 million tweets ("New Year's Eve Programming," 2015). Although social media is often abuzz for sport mega-events like the Super Bowl, the Olympics, and the Final Four, it is very much a factor in day-to-day sport news and regular-season contests.

WHY SOCIAL MEDIA?

Clearly, then, one answer for the question "Why should sport organizations be using social media?" is that the sheer volume of messages and audiences demands it. However, there are several other important reasons why sport organizations should not only be using social media but also have a plan to use it strategically.

Framing

Framing is derived from media research and suggests that the mass media shapes the ways audiences understand news stories by the language they use to report the story

(Kuypers & Cooper, 2005; Paxton, 2004; Tian & Stewart, 2005). More specifically, Entman (1993) contended that to frame is to "select some aspects of a perceived reality and make them more salient in a communicating text, in such a way to promote a particular problem definition, causal interpretation, moral evaluation, and/or treatment recommendation for the item described" (p. 52). While this capability has traditionally been squarely couched in the realm of the mass media, social media extends that same capability to users who can introduce their own framings of stories into the public discussion. For sport organizations, social media offers the ability to frame stories in particular ways and provides an outlet to counter inaccurate or unfavorable information that is being presented. Essentially, social media provides a way to say, "Here's our version of the story."

This messaging delivers information to fans and other stakeholders, who can then re-transmit or "share" that narrative, creating a spiral effect that exponentially increases the distribution of the narrative. As an example of how this can work, Sanderson (2008) investigated how Boston Red Sox pitcher Curt Schilling used his blog to counteract allegations that he had manufactured an injury during the 2004 American League Championship Series (ALCS). He found that Schilling used this platform to "turn the tables" on sport media members and become a sport media critic himself, presenting himself in a positive manner of which blog readers were overwhelmingly supportive. Put more simply: *If the sport organization does not tell its own story, someone else will.*

Feedback

Through social media, sport organizations have unprecedented avenues to connect and engage with fans and other stakeholders. Many sport organizations are taking advantage of social media to encourage fans to participate in promotions, to entice fans to attend games, and to obtain input from fans, all of which can then strengthen fans' identification with the team. One convenient way to obtain feedback is to simply ask questions. The Phoenix Suns are an organization that consistently does this on social media. For example, they have asked followers on Twitter what they think of upcoming line-ups.

These particular social media messages are convenient ways to cultivate fan identity and make fans feel more connected with the team. Such messages open up the potential for ongoing dialogue with fans. This is not to say that every single message has to be given a response (indeed this would be impossible for most sport organizations), but the important thing is to establish an *expectation* or a *culture of dialogue*. Social media can be useful as a vehicle to disseminate one-way information, but when the conversation becomes two-way, it increases social media's value exponentially. Organizational consultant Gary Heil has a succinct yet illustrative way of looking at organizational social media use: "Social media is only useful to the degree to which it is used to build and develop relationships" (personal communication, February 15, 2014). If there is minimal or no interaction and engagement on social media, it is very difficult for organizations to build and develop relationships.

In addition to fans, other stakeholder relationships can be developed via social media. The Phoenix Suns sometimes practice this by integrating sponsors like Verizon into their tweets and the Carolina Panthers promote playlists from players and coaches and mention Bose.

Certainly, there is a delicate balance to be struck here, as one stakeholder group (e.g., fans) could be turned off by a large dosage of these kinds of messages. However, placing sponsors into the social media content lineup is a great way to enhance partnerships with these important stakeholders.

Evolution of Communication

Communication is evolving at a rapid pace. Large amounts of information can be transmitted in seconds from nearly any location and people have access to a wealth of information via their mobile phones. As such, it is important for sport organizations to take a proactive, rather than a reactive, approach to social media plans. In other words, social media is always in a state of flux, and it is important for those who are responsible for social media plans to be aware of the latest developments and trends and to modify the social media plan accordingly. No doubt this is challenging. For example, those responsible for social media plans likely have other organizational responsibilities and it may be difficult to find the time to not only keep up to date on this information, but to also spend sufficient time learning the nuances of new platforms. Additionally, staying up to date on trends may render certain aspects of the organization's social media plan obsolete or necessitate a change in direction. Acknowledging these limitations, it is nevertheless essential to stay current on social media developments. Failing to maintain relevance with social media may cause the organization's social media efforts to appear stale to fans and other stakeholders may then migrate to organizations who maintain more interactive social media accounts. This potentially creates an image issue that the organization is "out of touch" and may cause the organization to fall behind competitors who are savvier in staying abreast of social media trends and developments. As platforms evolve and audiences migrate, it will be imperative for sport organizations to be aware of how these changes affect their social media plan.

Staying current on social media trends also is of particular importance to maintain credibility with athletes, who thus far, have generally been early adopters of emerging social media platforms. Therefore, if a sport organization is going to manage athletes' social media use, and have a plan in place for potential issues arising from their content, it is important to understand what platforms athletes are using and the manner in which they are being used. For example, younger people appear to be migrating away from Facebook (Matthews, 2014); thus, a high school athletic program or collegiate athletic program should incorporate this trend into plans for managing athletes' social media use and focus efforts on platforms that this cohort is prominently using (e.g., Instagram, Snapchat). The takeaway here is that social media plans should of necessity be flexible rather than static. A sport organization can maximize the potential of social media by taking on the challenge of recognizing and applying trends and developments to its plan.

There are, of course, a number of reasons sport organizations should pay close attention to social media, but these are some of the more significant areas of emphasis. One final point to stress is that *social media is not a fad*. True, platforms may come and go, but the underlying structure is too powerful to ever entirely evaporate. The capabilities are too immense. The ability to create and disseminate content is a benefit that most people are unlikely to give up in mass quantities. For sport organizations, the challenge is to optimize social media and use it as a resource to achieve goals. Just like any other key area of an organization that requires a plan, social media should not be left to chance. It is also important to remember that social media should not be seen as an entity in and of itself. Rather, it should run through every aspect of the sport organization and be a strand that connects the various units of the organization to one another and to external stakeholders all in the pursuit of organizational goals and relationship building.

CHAPTER QUESTIONS

If you worked for a sport organization and were asked by executives if the organization needed a social media plan, how would you respond?

_____

_____

_____

_____

_____

_____

_____

_____

_____

Do you follow any sport organizations on social media? If so, on what platforms? In your assessment, how capably are these organizations using social media?

_____

_____

_____

_____

_____

_____

_____

_____

_____

Is it important for sport organizations to engage and interact with fans on social media? Why or why not? If so, what platforms would be more optimal for this than others?

_____

_____

_____

_____

_____

_____

_____

_____

The chapter provides examples of the Phoenix Suns and Carolina Panthers integrating corporate sponsors into social media content. Do you think this is a good practice? Why or why not? What are some of the advantages and risks?

_____

_____

_____

_____

_____

_____

_____

_____

If you were in charge of creating a social media plan for a sport organization, what would be your goals for the plan?

_____

_____

_____

_____

_____

_____

_____

_____

INDUSTRY INTERVIEWS

Craig Pintens, Senior Associate Athletic Director—Marketing & Public Relations, University of Oregon

How is your organization trying to manage social media? How has social media affected/influenced your organization?

Social media is the biggest advancement in sports public relations since the Internet became commercialized in 1995. It provides an excellent two-way stream of information that keeps fans informed on your team(s). We have over 40 official social media accounts, which can be a very daunting task to manage. We do not have a person dedicated to social media; rather we make it a part of everyone's job in the marketing and athletic communications office. We feel everyone in our organization is responsible for social media. With over 200 employees and 500 student-athletes in the athletic department at the University of Oregon, those people are a key extension of our brand.

Why do sports organizations need a social media plan?

Planning is a key ingredient of any successful execution. A social media plan that contains your goals, mediums, and strategy will go a long way toward ensuring success.

What factors should be considered when making a social media plan?

- Resources—Are you going to be able to adequately staff your accounts to ensure success?
- Management—Who will administrate your accounts?
- Goals
- Software/Hardware needs
- Analytics
- How will you share your success?

Derrick Docket, Associate Commissioner of New Media and Technology, Missouri Valley Conference

How is your organization trying to manage social media? How has social media affected/influenced your organization?

As far as personnel, I'm the point person for our social media, and manage all accounts. I use some online tools to help with content management and analytics as well.

Social media has changed the way we communicate with our fans. We've done things to reward them for being a fan and interacting with us. We want to give our fans on social media the news and info, but also reward them for being fans. This includes chances to win tickets, participate and help us create content, and more.

Why do sports organizations need a social media plan?

It's important to have a social media plan for a number of reasons. Even though the outcome of the competition may dictate some of your content, it's important to remember that you're promoting and acting as the voice of a brand. Having a social media plan can help to maintain focus, especially if you're working as part of a team of social media managers.

What factors should be considered when making a social media plan?

- When making a social media plan, some of the things I like to take into consideration: Goals, Audience, Appropriate Platforms, Resources (budget/personnel), Tone/Voice
- What are my goals?
- Who is my target audience?
- What are the appropriate social media platforms for me to use?
- What are my resources to help? Budget restrictions? Do I have any additional manpower to help?
- What is the tone and voice I intend to use?

INTERVIEW QUESTIONS

Craig Pintens suggested that social media is the biggest advancement in public relations since the commercialization of the Internet. Do you agree? Why or why not?

_____

_____

_____

_____

_____

_____

_____

_____

Derrick Docket discussed how the Missouri Valley Conference uses social media to reward fans. Given that Docket works in collegiate athletics, do you think that is more appropriate for amateur sport organizations than professional? Why or why not? If you think rewarding fans should be part of a social media plan, what are some ways to do that?

_____

_____

_____

_____

_____
_____
_____
_____

Pintens suggested that athletic communication employees and student-athletes are an extension of the brand. How should that influence an organization's approach to a social media plan?

_____
_____
_____
_____
_____
_____
_____

The University of Oregon and the Missouri Valley Conference take different approaches to managing social media. Lists some reasons for having all staff members responsible (Oregon) or one point person (Missouri Valley Conference) along with factors that might influence the rationale for both approaches.

_____
_____
_____
_____
_____
_____

How would you determine a target audience for a sport organization's social media plan? Can there be more than one target audience? Why or why not?

_____
_____
_____
_____
_____
_____
_____

2

Developing a Comprehensive Plan

INTRODUCTION

Just like any organization, sport organizations are comprised of a variety of departments that collectively enable the organization to function. These departments include, among others, player personnel, ticketing, marketing, community relations, human resources, and public relations. Sport is somewhat unique when it comes to social media plans, because the level at which a sport organization participates (e.g., professional or amateur) is likely to influence how social media is used, which therefore affects the components of the plan. For example, an intercollegiate athletics department has to ensure that social media usage does not violate any National Collegiate Athletic Association (NCAA) rules, whereas this is not a concern for a professional sport organization.

As noted earlier, while social media may often be assigned to the communications department in a sport organization, to be fully optimized, it should run through all facets of the organization and not simply be viewed as something that is solely used for information dissemination. While information distribution is certainly one of the primary functions of social media, there is much more to it than that, especially if the organization wants to develop and strengthen relationships with stakeholder groups. To begin, there are a number of important questions that have to be answered, and the answers to such questions will be different based on the unique characteristics of each organization.

1. Who will be responsible for the social media plan?

While social media can, and should be, a participative endeavor within the sport organization, at some point there will have to be a point person, or a working group of individuals who will be responsible for the social media plan. There are a variety of factors that enter into this equation. Who "knows" social media? Who is familiar with the various platforms and understands the differences and similarities between them? These questions do not suggest that social media cannot be "learned," but ideally, the person/people put in charge of the social media plan understand its nuances and are capable of answering questions and explaining social media terminology to others in the organization who may not be familiar with it. Additionally, it is worth noting that the person/individuals should be able to articulate to others in the organization why it is important for the organization to be active in using social media, along with the value social media can provide. Ideally, the person/group selected will be active on at least several social media platforms and will have a history of responsible social media usage. It also is worth noting here that in the initial stages, it may be helpful to retain a consultant who can advise and guide the person or individuals through the process of creating a plan.

2. How will the organization use social media?

Once a decision has been made as to who will have responsibility for the social media plan, the next step involves analyzing all the various departments in the organization and determining if the organization will have "one" voice or if other departments will have a unique social media presence. For example, a professional sport team may have an "official" team account that posts information relating to game performance, personnel transactions, or other competition related events, whereas the organization's public relations department may have its own account that posts pertinent information related to that specific area of the organization. For example, the Carolina Panthers Public Relations Department maintains a Twitter account separate from the official team account. Their separate Twitter account once tweeted about player Greg Olson's son's heart defect being featured on an upcoming pregame show.

For an intercollegiate athletic department, where there are a diverse number of student-athletes participating in a variety of sports, each individual sport may have an individual account, while there also is a general athletic department account. For example, the University of Washington women's softball team maintains a distinct Instagram account from the University of Washington Athletics Instagram account where they post pictures highlighting things like the release of their 2015 schedule.

Regardless of the level at which a sport organization is participating, at some level, deciding who will operate social media accounts becomes a staffing issue. In regard to available time, it may not be feasible for one person to manage multiple organizational accounts, especially if there are several social media platforms involved. While it is true that content management services like Hootsuite simplify this process, there is still the question of how much one person can be expected to do, especially given the 24/7 news cycle of sport. This decision is also based on knowledge. For example, in an intercollegiate athletics program like men's golf, the sports information director may be better suited to run the social media accounts for that program, compared to, say, the chief sports information director, who may have limited involvement and interaction with the golf program due to other responsibilities.

© Rawpixelimages | Dreamstime.com

In most organizations, it is likely that there will be multiple accounts operated by different individuals; therefore, another important consideration is overlap. For instance, if the official team account is posting content related to game information, should the public relations account post similar content? Or will the public relations account differentiate itself by focusing more on promotional and personal-interest content? Certainly, there can be times where overlap occurs (e.g., significant accomplishments such as winning a championship) and organizations can share content in meaningful ways that do not overtly appear to overlap. One example of this overlap is a Clemson Athletics official Facebook account sharing the women's tennis team's Facebook post.

In general, however, if there is overlap in content, it will cause confusion among fans and may unnecessarily minimize audience size, as some people may perceive that they do not need to follow multiple accounts that are essentially providing the same information. It is also worth noting here that if an official organization account is using multiple social media platforms, to what extent will overlap occur between those different sites? For instance, if an organization is sharing the same photos on Instagram and Snapchat, is there really a need for a fan to follow the organization on both platforms? Some audience members may do so, simply out of devotion to the team, but it is ideal to have differentiation across platforms.

Although this will be detailed in a later chapter, another important consideration here involves how social media use by athletes, coaches, and other high-profile individuals in the organization factors into the plan. To what extent will these individuals receive education about social media and their involvement in promoting organization events? Additionally, will other people in the organization manage these accounts? If so, who will have that responsibility and what parameters will be put into place to guide content and posting frequencies? Deciding who is going to operate the various social media accounts is likely to be one of the more time-consuming tasks of the social media plan, but it is of critical importance.

3. What platforms will be used?

There are a number of social media platforms that a sport organization can utilize. Every organization is unique in the staffing resources that are available for social media and the financial commitment that can be made. Thus, which platforms are utilized will likely vary from one organization to the next, but in general, the key factor to consider in this particular phase is whether the organization will take a broad approach and be on every platform, or instead try to concentrate on a few select platforms. This decision ties into the earlier point about differentiating content by platforms. Some organizations may decide that focusing on two to three platforms makes sense for the resources they have. The benefit of this approach is that it allows an organization to cultivate proficiency on these particular platforms. This also can decrease staffing needs and increase efficiency if personnel are already stretched for time with other duties (in smaller sport organizations some people perform duties of several functional areas). The downside is that it can mean the organization is losing access to potential fans, customers, and other stakeholders who are using other platforms. On the flip side, a presence on multiple platforms can increase exposure to more stakeholder groups, but it may increase the chances of content overlap, create pressure to find consistently unique content, and stretch staffing resources. Interns are a potential solution in this respect, but it can be risky to empower an intern with responsibility for social media content. In such situations, interns should be carefully screened to minimize the potential for a public relations issue. This scrutiny is warranted because, unfortunately, many news outlets are eager to pounce on a social media misstep by a sport organization.

4. What are the goals for social media?

Social media is not something that should be left to chance or implemented on a whim. To be successful, it needs to be purposeful, goal-driven, and well thought out. There can be collective goals that shape overall social media usage, as well as individualized goals that are specific to each departmental account. *It is important to note here that social media goals should align with the overall goals of the organization.* The more these two align, the more effective it will be to measure the effectiveness of the social media plan and the return on investment that social media provides for the organization. Goals also may vary based on the type of platform being used. Following is a list of example goals that might comprise a social media plan:

Facebook:
- Post at least 10 content items each week, 8 of which will include a video or photo.
- Like 50% of user-generated positive comments.
- Respond to 25% of user-generated posts with positive, encouraging comments.

- For negative feedback, initiate steps to resolve issue, if feasible.
- Mention Facebook accounts of key partners (media, sponsors) at least once a week.

Twitter:
- Post at least 20 content items each week, 5 of which will include a video or photo.
- During games, tweet at least two questions to invite interaction with fans.
- Re-tweet 80% of mentions that reflect positively on the organization.
- Respond to 25% of tweets with positive, encouraging comments.
- Obtain a sponsor for season-long Twitter promotion.
- Integrate hashtags to enhance promotional efforts for organizational events and giveaways.

Instagram:
- Post at least 10 photos or videos each week.
- Identify at least one event each week where fans can be encouraged to submit photos.
- Reward at least 20 fans during the season for submitting compelling Instagram content and share this information across other organizational social media platforms.

Snapchat
- Post at least 20 snaps a week that focus on "insider access" (behind the scenes content that fans cannot obtain anywhere else).
- Identify at least one in-season promotion where fans can be encouraged to use Snapchat.
- Increase followers by 35% between opening and close of season.

Pinterest
- Develop five boards that are tied to distinct aspects of the organization:
  - Tailgating
  - Merchandise
  - In-game experience
  - Community Relations
  - Facility/Venue
- Reward at least 15 fans who re-pin content with merchandise.
- Increase followers by 20% from beginning to end of season.

With goal setting, it is crucial that goals be measurable. For example, having a goal of "increasing Twitter followers" is vague, as even an increase of one follower would, theoretically, achieve the goal. Setting specific goals will assist in the assessment and modification of the social media plan. Specific and concrete goals also help guide usage by providing a purpose for each post. For instance, those responsible for posting can ask, "Will this post help meet the goal?" Content that does not relate back to a goal should be avoided or changed so that it does meet the goal.

5. How often will we implement and assess the plan?

These factors will be covered in later chapters in the text, but it is important to discuss them in the planning phase. It is ideal that a plan be assessed in regular intervals, and that there be a procedure in place to handle breaking news, or other incidents that transpire quickly; this way, the organization's social media efforts are flexible and not tied down by bureaucracy. This also helps with accountability, as those employees who will be evaluated on social media effectiveness will know the criteria by which they will be measured. This helps avoid situations where organization members are lax with responsibilities because they believe no one will notice.

In summary, for sport organizations to have social media work strategically and effectively, there has to be a clear plan to guide its use. This requires a significant devotion of time and effort, but the payoff is worth this initial investment. It also is important to note here that while sport organizations can learn from one another (and indeed, social media becomes a great source of collective intelligence in sport), trying to mimic another sport organization is likely to prove ineffective. Every sport organization is unique and has a different culture and fans—a fact that should be embraced. Clearly, learning from another organization and incorporating those ideas into the social media plan can be very beneficial; however, outright replication is not the way to achieve success in social media.

CHAPTER QUESTIONS

Why is it important for social media usage to be purposeful?

_____

_____

_____

_____

_____

_____

_____

_____

_____

If you were in charge of selecting someone to develop a social media plan for a sport organization, what qualifications would you look for? Why?

_____
_____
_____
_____
_____
_____
_____
_____
_____

Research sport organization directories and identify someone who is responsible for social media content. What kind of qualifications and experiences do they have?

_____
_____
_____
_____
_____
_____
_____
_____
_____

Is it important for sport organizations to assess the personal usage of someone they are considering to run organization accounts? Why or why not? Are there any ethical issues with this?

_____
_____
_____
_____
_____
_____
_____
_____
_____

Is it important that organizations not overlap between accounts and platforms? Why or why not?

_____

_____

_____

_____

_____

_____

_____

_____

What kinds of sport organizations would benefit from having a presence on several platforms? What kinds of sport organizations would benefit from having a presence on every platform?

_____

_____

_____

_____

_____

_____

_____

_____

INDUSTRY INTERVIEWS

Carter Henderson, Associate Athletic Director for Public Relations & Communications, University of Washington

What functions or departments of the sport organization should be involved in a social media plan?

Any and all who have a desire to use social media. Followers have demonstrated insatiable appetites to see what happens behind the scenes at sports organizations, from the grounds crew to coaching staffs and everyone in between. As long as the content stays on-brand and on-message, social media provides an easy way to form and deepen connections between sports organizations and our fans. We cast a wide net when crafting our social media plan, and aim to make it applicable to any units within our organization who have an interest to use it.

Is social media something "separate" from the rest of the organization, or is it something that should cut across all aspects of the organization?

We view social media as a vehicle to deliver the overall brand messaging of the organization. When it's working properly, it feels exactly like the same voice the organization uses throughout all other external touch points, and weaves seamlessly into everything we do.

Who should have primary responsibility for developing and overseeing a social media plan in a sport organization?

Ideally, an integrated marketing and communications team. It's easy for social media to drift too far into the marketing shop (think 2-for-1 ticket offers) or too far into the communications shop (think bland press release regurgitations). We strive for a balance between the two that speaks as an authentic voice of our brand. Regardless of who sets and executes the vision, the social properties need to look, feel, and sound like all other communications emanating from the organization.

Should a sport organization take a broad approach and be on every social media platform, or should it try and specialize on a small number of platforms?

I believe strongly that organizations should target only the social mediums they believe are going to yield the most effective progress toward achieving their overall marketing and communications objectives. It's easy to fall into the trap of believing that social media resources (largely time and energy) are infinite, but any of us who have overreached learn quickly that social resources are exhausted very quickly. At Washington, we try to master a few platforms rather than settling for a diluted presence on all social media channels.

How important is it that content be unique and differentiated on each social media platform, or is it okay that content be duplicated on social media platforms?

I think it depends on the situation and the content. We segment each social media platform by audience, so in situations where the messaging hierarchy is the same for multiple audiences, it's appropriate for the content to be the same. We've had instances, like the hiring of a new head football coach, where the content we produced across all mediums shared the same aesthetic and messaging. We've also had times when we've segmented messaging to different targets.

Kelly Mosier, Director of Digital Communications, University of Nebraska

What functions or departments of the sport organization should be involved in a social media plan?

Social media is an extension of an organization's communications and branding plan. From that standpoint, everyone needs to have a hand in that planning. On the flip side, social media has its own challenges to other types of communication, so specific social media plans should be spearheaded by someone who prioritizes to social media and content creators for that plan.

Is social media something separate from the rest of the organization, or is it something that should cut across all aspects of the organization?

Social media cuts across everyone, on some level. Most employees will have social media accounts. Even if they're private accounts, they still represent the organization to their circle of friends. That being said, I think the people who run brand accounts need self-autonomy from the rest of the department because they will need to make editorial decisions about content timing and need to be able to make those decisions without pressure from other departments.

Who should have primary responsibility for developing and overseeing a social media plan in a sport organization?

Organizations are best served by having an independent director overseeing social media. That person ideally is involved with the overall digital plan for the organization.

Should a sport organization take a broad approach and be on every social media platform, or should they try to specialize on a smaller number of platforms?

Both and neither. Organizations shouldn't spread themselves too thin across platforms they can't create consistent content for; at the same time they shouldn't be afraid to try new things that might not be totally formed yet.

How important is it that content be unique and differentiated on each social media platform, or is it okay that content be duplicated on social media platforms?

Good content is good content regardless of platform. Some content will perform better on some platforms than other platforms, but that's more of a point of strategy across different platforms and implementation versus true differences in content. I'd also differentiate engagement vs. content. There are engagement strategies that could also be considered content, but those don't translate across platforms very well, if at all.

INTERVIEW QUESTIONS

Carter Henderson noted that Washington hiring a new coach was one occasion where social media content was duplicated across platforms. Can you think of other examples where duplication across social media would be viable for a sport organization?

_____

_____

_____

_____

_____

_____

_____

How can those responsible for a social media plan ensure that social media delivers the overall brand messaging of the organization?

_____

_____

_____

_____

_____

_____

_____

Kelly Mosier suggested that organizations are best served by having an independent social media director. Do you agree? Why or why not?

_____

_____

_____

_____

_____

_____

_____

_____

Mosier also talked about the difference between engagement and content. What is the difference between those two and how might the social media platform being used dictate that difference?

_____

_____

_____

_____

_____

_____

_____

_____

3

Social Media Use by Coaches and Administrators

> "IF ATHLETICS IS THE FRONT PORCH OF A UNIVERSITY, THEN SOCIAL MEDIA IS THE FRONT LAWN—KEEP IT CLEAN."
>
> *Chris Yandle*

Social media has officially crept its way into our DNA. Not only does it define us personally and professionally, but it also is the benchmark by which sport organizations are measured. Are you good or bad at social media? Does it have a direct or indirect correlation to wins and losses on the field of competition?

Now, more than ever, administrators and coaches are visible public figures. Before the advent of social media—and email for that matter—athletic directors, coaches, general managers, and other organization leaders were able to navigate the trials and tribulations of the sport business behind relatively closed doors, without being under the constant scrutiny of the media and fans. In today's sport landscape, scrutiny is at every corner. With every bad play, bad game, or bad season, fans covet that immediate access to athletes (including student-athletes), coaches, and administrators. *But what they perhaps covet the most is an immediate answer.* With 140 characters and the push of a button, they can now sound off on suspecting (and unsuspecting) subjects—whether they called the last play that resulted in a loss, or if they selected what the vocal fan base viewed as a "bad hire." Whatever the reason may be, administrators and coaches are now on call 24 hours a day. No longer are their scheduled news conferences once a week; they are now all day every day because social media is—in fact—a 24-hour news conference that never goes dark.

How have administrators and coaches handled this newfound responsibility of proper (and immediate) social media use? For the vast majority of Division I athletics, the results have been extremely mixed. Posts have included official breaking coaching news: "In November 2011, Arizona AD Greg Byrne tweeted an announcement of the new coach and his family, linking to a photo of Rich Rodriguez and his family."

A year later, Texas Tech AD Kirby Hocutt (@kirbyhocutt) tweeted a similar message to announce the Red Raiders' new head football coach. When readers clicked on the link, a picture of Texas Tech alum Kliff Kingsbury appeared, signaling his arrival as the new head football coach.

Breaking news in this manner gives fans "exclusive" insider access (Kassing & Sanderson, 2010) into how sport organizations decide to announce personnel transactions. Traditionally, the media is alerted and the beat writer then writes a column on the new coach. With Byrne and Hocutt, everyone received the news at the same time: media, alumni, and fans were all on the same level playing field.

Twitter also has been the source of brokering home-and-home football series between two athletic directors. In what is believed to the first scheduling protocol of its kind, Kansas State University Athletic Director John Currie (@John_Currie) and Mississippi State University Athletic Director Scott Stricklin (@stricklinMSU) worked out a deal that included a game in Manhattan, Kansas, in 2018 and in Starkville, Mississippi, in 2019. From an outsider's perspective, nothing was planned beforehand. This exchange began as a challenge from Currie to participate in "Chillin' For Charity," which raises money for breast cancer research and benefits the Kay Yow Foundation. As one of the people challenged by  Currie in the video, Stricklin saw it as an opportunity for the schools to play each other.

Stricklin offered an initial deal for a home-and-home, but those dates didn't match up for Kansas State. So Currie offered a counter-deal and Stricklin accepted. Deal done. All over Twitter.

The idea of scheduling a home-and-home series on Twitter happened organically. Fans want to be engaged and love seeing this type of interaction between collegiate athletic directors. Twenty years ago, fans were not privy to how scheduling worked in college football. Thanks to Currie and Stricklin, the curtain was pulled back for all to see, for what has all the makings of a great college football series (McMurphy, 2014).

Crowdsourcing is another excellent benefit offered by social media. Crowdsourcing involves a person or an organization posing a question or problem to digital "crowds" and obtaining responses from these individuals. For example, a sport organization might send out a tweet asking fans to vote on several different uniform combinations for an upcoming game. In doing so, an organization provides a unique opportunity to engage fans as well as get important marketing information that can inform other organizational aspects such as merchandising. Fans want a chance to be a part of their favorite sports team. When a sport organization wants to solicit feedback and input, there is no better approach than going straight to its loudest and proudest stakeholders: the fans. Let's go back to Arizona Athletic Director Greg Byrne, who gave Wildcats fans an important feedback opportunity about the logo on the new football video board in June 2014 when he tweeted three pictures of the video board with different logos and asked what fans thought.

Ross Bjork, the Athletic Director at the University of Mississippi, used crowdsourcing in a fun way after Mississippi defeated the University of Alabama on October 3, 2014. At the time, Alabama was the #1 team in college football. After the game, fans were quite jubilant and tore down the goal posts at Vaught-Hemingway stadium. As a result, the University of Mississippi was fined $50,000 by the Southeastern Conference (SEC). Bjork decided to use Twitter to (jokingly) crowdsouce donations to pay the fine.

Although done for humor, a website raised over $85,000 within three days after Bjork's tweet (Ortiz Jr., 2014). Taking this example and applying it to a social media plan suggests that something as simple as asking fans for their opinion on a logo on a scoreboard is all it may take to hook them into your social media strategy.

When an organization has a leader like Currie, Stricklin, or Byrne using Twitter in these ways, other organization staff and coaches will soon follow suit—and a social media culture is cultivated. The ability to see the personality of a sport organization's coaches and staff is another element that factors into social media usage. Often, through the lens of traditional media, we see a very scripted version of administrators and coaches. While that is understandable, as coaches and administrators do not want to make missteps that could harm the team, it also hinders fans' ability to connect with them—and social media can remedy that situation. Through social media, administrators can express opinions, convey gratitude to fans, and comment on other sport topics/non-sports topics. This provides opportunities for fans to identify with them, which can potentially enhance support for the coach, administrator, and organization.

How do those responsible for a social media plan in sport organizations get "buy-in" from administrators, coaches, and staff? Their voices must be included in the social media plan. They cannot be on the outside looking in; instead they must be on the inside looking out into the crowd, sharing their views and their stories. An example of this buy-in came with the University of Miami initiating its "Building Champions" campaign, which was a three-year initiative developed by the Hurricane Club to grow its membership base and expand its national reach. That reach expanded to social media as Miami coaches, staff, student-athletes, administrators, and alumni began tweeting positive UM news with the #BuildingChampions hashtag.

"#BuildingChampions was a branding initiative to capture and embody what we do within the University of Miami Athletics Department," according to Jesse Marks, Associate Athletic Director for Development at Miami. "Using the hashtag #BuildingChampions not only drove participation in our Hurricane Club, but it gave identity to all the great things our student-athletes and department were accomplishing."

As the #BuildingChampions hashtag and campaign began to build steam, Miami staff began to capture those successes on the field through the power of social media. It was in the email signatures of all department staff members. With the success of the campaign, department-wide buy-in came and trickled into the UM fan and alumni communities.

With Miami's department-wide social success with #BuildingChampions, Marks believes that more development offices will go to this type of social reach. "Of course," Marks observed, "athletics development offices must increase their reach across all mediums—both traditional and nontraditional. Social (media) is one—if not, the most—important piece of the overall strategy."

Miami's "Building Champions" campaign was so successful that Marks and another staff member won not one but two Bronze Telly Awards. "This is just the tip of the iceberg for us," Marks said. "As technology evolves, we will see less friction in digital giving and more data and tracking services. We need to have the mechanism/technology to tell a story and securely capture the impulse digital donor." Professional and collegiate athletes can easily network and pose for photo opportunities, including using each other's organizational hashtags in social media posts.

Beyond initiating organization-wide hashtags, another way to cultivate social media culture involves adding social media suites and fan teams to magnify the fan's voice (such as the San Francisco Giants social media café in AT&T Stadium). In another example, for three games during the 2013 football season, the Miami Hurricanes launched the @USocialSuite, which was a place for selected fans and non-credentialed bloggers to share their unique experiences inside Sun Life Stadium. The concept, which was a hybrid of the Cleveland Indians' Social Media Suite and the University of California's "Blog From the Fog," was developed by Chris Yandle while he was at Miami, and a year later, he developed the #SocialSwarm Fan Team at Georgia Tech. #SocialSwarm and other fan-centric programs like it were developed in order to grow relationships between the Georgia Tech Athletic Association and its various social influences. #SocialSwarm is a place for fan ambassadors to share their unique views throughout the stadium in-game and engage with other Georgia Tech fans, students, and alumni. Programs such as these provide an additional layer to a sport organization's social media presence, as well as show fans that the organization does care about them, what they say, and that the organization is listening.

In essence, a social media plan/strategy is only going to succeed if listening to fans is a priority. Said differently, there needs to be an emphasis on including fans' voice and creating opportunities for engagement and participation. Administrators can share great information, but if they are only shouting through a megaphone and not engaging with fans and other stakeholders, then there is really no plan at all.

To garner complete buy-in from all relevant organizational personnel, consider these three things:

1. **The end goal.** Do you want be an information source? Do you want to crowd-source projects within the organization? How do your coaches want to use social media? (In collegiate athletics social media has become a very viable recruiting tool.)

2. **Be creative.** Encourage staff to be creative. Do not be a static billboard of tweets and posts.

3. **Support and listen.** Be a cheerleader for the organization and staff. But, most importantly, listen to what is being said about the organization.

The sport industry has been extremely quick to embrace technology. Further, it is the sport industry's application of technological change that has made its social media popularity skyrocket; in turn, this popularity has made it vital for coaches and administrators to keep pace.

CHAPTER QUESTIONS

How would you convince a coach or sport administrator to use social media?

_____

_____

_____

_____

_____

_____

_____

_____

For administrators and coaches who do use social media, how active should they be? Is it important that they be authentic, or is it fine for someone else to run the account?

_____

_____

_____

_____

_____

_____

_____

Are there some social media platforms that are more optimal for sport administrators and coaches? If so, what are they?

_____

_____

_____

_____

_____

_____

_____

_____

What other ways might administrators and coaches use social media to crowdsource?

_____

_____

_____

_____

_____

_____

_____

How does an administrator or coach "listen" to fans on social media?

_____

_____

_____

_____

_____

_____

_____

How might fan-driven social media programs—@USocialSuite and #SocialSwarm—benefit a sport organization? What challenges might prevent some sport organizations from implementing these kinds of programs?

_____

_____

_____

_____

_____

_____

_____

INDUSTRY INTERVIEWS

Chris Williams, Athletic Director, Southern Wesleyan University

Why should an administrator (athletic director, general manager) or coach use social media?

It provides free advertising and a way for you as the leader to send a message about your school. It gives an inside look into your world!

How would you "sell" a coach or administrator on using social media?

Recruit using the medium of the student-athlete. Also, help your current student-athletes learn how to better use the medium.

Are there particular social media platforms that make more sense for an administrator or coach to use?

Twitter, Facebook, and Instagram seem to be slightly more 'professional' platforms right now. Twitter seems to be the 'hot' spot for leaders to share ideas, thoughts, trends, and is a resource area for me as a leader to learn what others are doing at their campus.

Is it important for administrators or coaches to post their own content on social media? In other words, if someone else posts the content for them, does that matter? Why or why not?

I like to see 'your' words and thoughts. I do feel that a personal touch makes it very engaging and 'real'!

Kirby Garry, Director of Athletics, California State—Monterey Bay

Why should an administrator (athletic director, general manager) or coach use social media?

Social media provides access to the world. Social media platforms are essentially free tools to listen, learn, communicate, and market your personal or organization's story to the world. I feel like the days are gone as to *why*? . . . knowledge, understanding, and the basic skills sets needed to embrace social media are not optional for today's leaders. The question then shifts to strategy and tactics . . . not *if* you are on social media, but how are you going to utilize the power of social media.

How would you "sell" a coach or administrator on using social media?

*Legendary jazz musician Art Blakely once said, "If you're not appearing, you're disappearing." I think that says it all. College athletics is a competitive game, regardless

*h/t Garr Reynolds (@presentationzen)

of level, and if you are not on social media and utilizing the power of storytelling, branding, and marketing that can be accomplished on these platforms, then somebody else is and they are winning.

I would also add that if you are not telling your story on social media—then somebody else is . . . (telling your story). And you are losing control of your brand . . . that can be personal or organizational. That goes more into the power of listening, networking, engaging, providing customer service, etc. on social platforms.

And another thing I can't emphasize enough is the professional development aspect of social media . . . the networking and learning opportunities that can be discovered via social . . . I can honestly say I owe much of my personal growth, career development, and most recent opportunity to serve as an AD to the power of listening and learning from social media.

Are there particular social media platforms that make more sense for an administrator or coach to use?

Personally, Twitter and Instagram because of the one-to-one opportunities. And I would say Twitter first and foremost because it is a live play-by-play of what is going on in the world. We need to be in the know.

Then I think it's about personal and/or organizational strategy. The choice of platform can be decided on the demographic of the audience you are trying to reach. I'm a big believer in Gary Vaynerchuk's philosophy around "respecting the psychology of the platform" . . . it's not one size fits all.

It's not really about what my favorite platform is . . . it's about where my audience is. And that lends itself to basic fundamentals of communication and marketing . . . *know your audience*, right? Now you don't just have to know your audience . . . you need to know where your audience is . . . what platform they are on.

Is it important for administrators or coaches to post their own content on social media? In other words, if someone else posts the content for them, does that matter? Why or why not?

I believe in transparency and authenticity as a leader—and I embrace that on social media as well, again, because social media is the tool. I need to be me—whether in person or online.

I do see value in capitalizing on celebrity status of a social media account. The power of influence is very strong when follower numbers and reach is significant. The time demands on folks at the highest level are through the roof. So in that respect, I see value having a strategy around "voice" and content being shared.

All that said, I feel the most powerful social media influencers—as coaches and administrators—are those who are posting themselves and being authentic. The fans and followers acknowledge, appreciate, and are attracted by that in the end.

INTERVIEW QUESTIONS

Chris Williams suggested that one way to sell a coach on using social media is to "recruit using the medium of the student-athlete." Is social media an essential part of recruiting strategy?

_____

_____

_____

_____

_____

_____

_____

_____

Williams discussed that it's important for sport administrators to utilize a personal touch in their social media posts. How would you work with a coach or administrator who expressed skepticism about sharing their feelings on social media?

_____

_____

_____

_____

_____

_____

_____

_____

Kirby Garry indicated that he was a big advocate of professional development that occurred via social media. How does social media provide professional development and networking opportunities?

_____

_____

_____

_____

_____

_____

_____

_____

Garry indicated that transparency was an important characteristic for a leader in a sport organization. How can social media be used to convey transparency for leaders who work in sport organizations?

_____

_____

_____

_____

_____

_____

_____

_____

4

Social Media Use by Athletes

How powerful is social media? Derek Jeter announced his retirement from baseball following the 2014 season . . . on his Facebook page. *He* controlled the message. *He* did it on his own terms. Fans were able to hear it straight from the source, not a media report.

As the Jeter example indicates, *athletes can be their own media and control their own message.* This exponentially increases the audience size. In early 2015, Jeter's resignation letter had 76,484 likes and 56,370 shares.

Social media is still a relatively young medium, but in that short time frame no group has arguably endured more scrutiny online than athletes. High school, college, or professional athlete, it does not matter—fans, critics, and cynics now have unprecedented access to athletes, all within the click of a button and a string of 140 characters. As a result, sport organization coaches and administrators are sometimes faced with headlines like these, "Roddy White Reacts Harshly To George Zimmerman Verdict On Twitter" and "Cardale Jones: Classes Pointless" when athletes make politically charged statements or comments about his/her scholastic institution. (Huffington Post Sports, 2013; ESPN, 2012).

While there are certainly some athletes who do not use social media, a vast majority of athletes are using at least one platform (likely multiple), and athletes are starting at younger ages to use them, some starting as young as elementary school. Social media is a staple of athletes' everyday lives, and often times, content that an athlete believes to be acceptable becomes a problem once the spotlight increases. As one example of how embedded social media usage is among athletes, Browning and Sanderson (2012) interviewed Division I student-athletes about their use of Twitter, and many of them reported that they could not count the number of times they checked Twitter daily, because they were *always* checking their phone to see what updates had been posted and/or to see if their name had been mentioned. In the same study, they also discovered that for some student-athletes, checking Twitter was the first thing they did immediately after a game, and that some even checked their Twitter mentions at halftime.

What role should athletes play in social media strategy? Some organizations opt to keep their athletes out of the strategy, while some embrace them within it. As one example, the University of Washington (UW) selected 10 student-athletes to promote through branded Twitter accounts on GoHuskies.com. UW built a branded area for their student-athletes to build their online persona, and also educated them on proper and strategic social media use.

Some coaches go as far as implementing social media bans to keep their players from getting into trouble on social media. However, this does not always prevent incidents. In September 2014, Florida State University (FSU) quarterback and reigning Heisman Trophy winner Jameis Winston got in trouble because of social media . . . but not because he was using it. Florida State head coach Jimbo Fisher bans his players from

© Dolgachov | Dreamstime.com

using social media in-season. But Winston got a one-game suspension and made front-page headlines for what he said in a public forum that was relayed on Twitter.

Winston shouted a popular Internet meme in the heart of FSU's campus: "F*ck her right in the p****." He shouted it, and FSU students walking in the vicinity heard the awful remark, tweeted it, then the media picked up on it. As irony would have it, Florida State fans' ire was directed at the students who tweeted the comments, not at Winston. Although Florida State had instituted a Twitter restriction, when their quarterback opted to shout an inappropriate statement in a public forum without using social media, with the aid of social media, consequences resulted.

In a social media world, everyone is a reporter, everything is on record, and anything you say can be tweeted or posted online by someone within earshot of you. Is that fair? Maybe. Maybe not. But that is our digital society.

Given how quickly social media has proliferated, athletes are persistently getting in trouble for social media posts. For example, in 2012, the University of North Alabama removed a football player after he tweeted a racially charged message directed at President Obama (Schwab, 2012). That same year, the University of Michigan ended their recruitment of Yuri Wright after he posted a series of lewd and misogynistic tweets. Wright also was expelled from his high school ("Recruit Yuri Wright expelled for tweets," 2012). This particular case is interesting because Wright's Twitter account was private. For some athletes, there is an illusion of privacy on social media, but even on private accounts, once a message is sent, ownership is lost, and all it takes is one of these followers or friends to share the content publicly and it can never be retrieved.

Social media can—and should—be a place for athletes to spread social good and positive stories. There are moments of athletes visiting children's hospitals or doing community service—not because they have to, but because they want to. Unfortunately, social good like this does not move the needle in the media, and so it is rarely covered. Tweets go largely unnoticed until they become newsworthy, often for something that is considered to create controversy. This generally involves tweets that include racist, homophobic, and/or misogynistic language, a tweet that is perceived to be a criticism of a coach or teammate, or an attack on a sport media member. In some cases, an athlete may have a history of responsible social media usage, but this can be dwarfed by one mistake that often lives on in infamy. Consider the earlier example of the Ohio State quarterback Cardale Jones's tweet about coming to school to play football and not attend classes. During the 2014 college football season, Jones, who began the season as the third-string quarterback, found himself inserted into the starting lineup as Ohio State entered the Big 10 Championship after the first and second string quarterbacks sustained season-ending injuries. When this news broke, Jones's tweet from two years prior found its way into many of the news reports about his ascension to the starting quarterback position before arguably the biggest game of the season. Social media misuse can easily send an athlete from the penthouse to the doghouse in a hurry. By including them in the overall social media plan, a sport organization can help combat negative outcomes.

The degree to which athletes will be allowed to use social media or to which their social media content will be incorporated is an important element of the social media plan. This is more of an issue in amateur athletics, because it would be difficult for a professional team to ban use of a particular social media outlet, although professional league rules do prohibit social media usage during a specified time period before a game, during a game, and after a game, continuing through post-game media interviews. At the amateur level, there are a variety of perspectives on both sides of the argument about social media restrictions for student-athletes. Some of these are summarized below.

RESTRICTING USE

- **Eliminating Distractions:** If athletes are restricted from using social media, this enhances their ability to focus on game preparation and avoid unnecessary media and public relations incidents stemming from the media reporting about an athlete's social media post. It should be noted, however, that these restrictions generally govern the posting of messages, so athletes are often still checking social media; they are just not transmitting messages.
- **Organization Protection:** By restricting athletes from using social media, the organization has greater control over messaging and can prevent sensitive information getting out that could create issues for the organization. As one noteworthy example, in 2009, Minnesota Timberwolves player Kevin Love tweeted out that head coach Kevin McHale had been let go by the organization, yet the team had not made any formal announcement, and was subsequently barraged by reporters trying to confirm this information ("Love: McHale won't return," 2009).

- **Athlete Protection:** There has been a growing trend of fans sending hateful messages to athletes via social media, primarily through Twitter. Given the content of these messages, it has been speculated that this constitutes a form of cyberbullying and can lead to mental health issues for athletes (Olson, 2013). Thus, by restricting social media usage, players may be spared reading these messages, which can come with alarming frequency. For example, Sanderson and Truax (2014) investigated tweets sent to University of Alabama kicker Cade Foster after the Auburn/Alabama game in November 2013, when he missed three field goals in his teams narrow loss to its rival, and found that from the time period of the kickoff to 24 hours later, Foster's account was mentioned in just over 12,000 tweets! With that being said, restricting social media does not necessarily prevent athletes from reading these messages. Thus, it is important that there be measures in place to help athletes deal with hateful messages, a topic we discuss later in the chapter.

- **Organization Harmony:** At times, athletes may post information on social media that can affect team camaraderie and draw the ire of the public. Sanderson (2013) noted that via social media, athletes are able to express more aspects of their personality, and while this can generally be a positive outcome, it also can result in athletes weighing in on sensitive issues that can prompt backlash. For instance, in 2011, Pittsburgh Steelers running back Rashard Mendenhall posted comments on Twitter questioning the public celebration of Osama Bin Laden's death and speculating that the 9/11 terrorist attacks were potentially a conspiracy. In response, Steelers president Art Rooney II issued a statement that expressed support for the military and indicated that it was difficult to comprehend what Mendenhall was thinking ("Rashard Mendenhall doesn't hold back," 2011).

ALLOWING USE

- **Enhancing Organization Visibility and Promotion:** In most cases, athletes possess significant audience followings on social media, and some may have a bigger audience than official organization accounts. Thus, organizations can enhance their reach by incorporating the player's social media accounts into organization events and encouraging players to promote them via social media. As this happens, the organization's reach broadens and there are more opportunities to reach fans and other stakeholders. The Golden State Warriors is one organization that actively promotes its athletes on social media. The team started an event to correspond with the opening of the season termed #TweediaDay, and actively encourages fans to send questions for players. The athletes answered fan questions, demonstrating that the key element of this promotion was successful.

- **Cultivating Responsible Social Media Habits:** For athletes who are in school, social media can be part of the educational experience. One criticism of banning social media is that this step is often taken without first providing education that lets athletes know where the boundaries lie. This critique emphasizes the need for athletes to be taught how social media can be used in ways that can benefit them. For instance, athletes can use social media to create a personal brand and to connect with potential mentors and other key individuals who can be of assistance to them. Social media—when used properly—can be a powerful tool to establish, solidify, and expand an athlete's personal brand. With a well-established brand in place, an athlete can utilize his or her social media channels as a vessel to share information about community service activities, have one-on-one connections with fans, and share amazing stories on a personal level. Social media has now become a major part of most organizations. Whether a college athlete goes on to play professional sports or enters another employment sector, social media is very likely going to be a part of that phase of their life. Accordingly, why not utilize their time in school to teach them about these particular aspects of social media?

- **Overall Number of Problematic Social Media Posts:** Athletes can create controversy with one social media post. This content sometimes becomes a major news story, which creates a negative domino effect. Fans can begin to form negative perceptions about athletes using social media and lump all athletes into one category. While it is important to acknowledge the risk that does come with social media, when considering the entire population of athletes who use social media and the number of posts they generate, the number of problematic incidents is plausibly a small percentage of those posts. In other words, while there are many athletes who do use social media responsibly, the frequency of media attention that is generally focused on the negative incidents may create perceptions that all athletes do on social media is create issues. To some extent, mistakes can be attributed to the newness of the medium. As users become more familiar with the norms and expectations for using social media (e.g., not sharing every feeling/thought, avoiding problematic language, using social media purposefully and to achieve goals), this can help correct problematic behavior (e.g., getting into arguments with fans/other players, posting insensitive comments that may have racial and/or homophobic overtones). To be sure, there will continue to be incidents, but education (something we discuss in more detail later) can be helpful in minimizing these occurrences.

- **Team Harmony:** Given how many athletes use social media as part of their social life, it can potentially be a source of conflict between athletes and coaches and potentially between athletes if social media restrictions are put in place and may erode any goodwill that the athlete feels towards the or-  ganization. For example, an athlete may perceive that the coach or team administrator is trying to censor his/her speech, or may perceive that they are being punished for the actions of another teammate. In the latter case, this creates the possibility of fostering animosity and discord among teammates, which may then affect in-game performance. As previously stated, there are arguments for implementing these restrictions, but this information should be conveyed in a way that will help athletes understand why this step is being taken. Overall, social media can be a commonality that draws players closer together. The coach also can be part of this equation by using social media, which can provide a point of connection between coach and players. This is of particular value in the recruiting process, given how many prospective student-athletes are using social media, and can be a way for a coach to gain an advantage. Finally, enabling players to use social media conveys an attitude of trust. Consider this comment from former University of Oregon football coach Chip Kelly:

> "If they can't be responsible in social media, then we recruited the wrong kids," Kelly said. "I think it's very prominent this day in age . . . and we try to educate our kids like we educate them in everything they do. But if you can't trust a kid on Twitter . . . can you trust them on third down?" (Jude, 2012)

Relationships between athletes and coaches are often predicated on trust. For Chip Kelly, this trust also extends to behavior away from the game and in this specific case, encompasses online behavior. Kelly's position also emphasizes that it may be prudent to trust players on social media, unless they provide reasons for that trust to be revoked.

EDUCATION

Education for high school and college students has now expanded beyond the classroom and playing fields. A need for education now exists in the digital media arena as kids—younger by the day—become immersed in social media. It has permeated our culture so much so that a post can be the lead story on the 6 o'clock evening news. Or better yet, an athlete's post can be dissected over and over and over again on a variety of sports talk shows on websites and 24-hour networks.

Believe it or not, social media is still in its infancy stages. Indeed, Facebook is only 10 years old, and some platforms such as Instagram and Snapchat are younger than five years old. Compare that to radio and television, mass communication platforms that have a much longer history, and the evolution that has occurred with those mediums. Given their youth, many people are still trying to comprehend social media, and as technology continues to evolve at a rapid pace, it can feel as though there is little time to master one social media platform before a new one emerges. With that context provided, it should perhaps not be surprising that we still hear about an athlete making an insensitive comment on Twitter, or posting a provocative photo on Instagram. Thus, it is crucial that education and training be provided to equip athletes with the tools to succeed at social media.

Why Social Media Education is Essential

After a practice, game, or a team meeting, athletes pick up their phones—not to call their mom or text their girlfriend or boyfriend—but to check (most likely) Twitter and see what is happening. In the case of an athlete making a game-winning shot or scoring the go-ahead touchdown, his or her Twitter timeline will be flooded with jubilation and congratulatory tweets. And if the athlete misses four field goals in a game? That athlete is forced to go into exile because of death threats, vitriol, or hateful tweets spewed towards him or her.

Unfortunately, this is not just limited to athletes, but also now includes their families. One of the more notable cases involved Kristen Blake, wife of NBA player Steve Blake. In 2012, Blake missed a potential game-winning shot at the end of regulation in Game 2 of the Western Conference Finals against the Oklahoma City Thunder. After the game, Kristen Blake started receiving criticism via Twitter; one particular message stated, "I hope your family gets murdered" (McMenamin, 2012).

Whether an organization elects to put restrictions on athletes' social media usage, education is an important part of any plan. Athletes receive media training that teaches them how to prepare themselves and succeed in traditional media interviews. Social media training is equally important, especially as athletes become their own media channels through these platforms. Additionally, unlike traditional media interviews, which sport organizations have a high degree of control over (e.g., making certain players available, scheduling time and location) with social media, athletes can post messages from any location, at any time, most likely through their mobile phone. Given this lack of control, it is imperative that social media education be provided on a consistent basis. There are several important factors that enter into the equation when formulating social media education:

© Pressureua | Dreamstime.com

How consistent will the education be?
Often, social media education is part and parcel of a host of other training programs that athletes receive prior to the beginning of the season. It may be important to provide periodic updates to athletes, as they are trying to process large quantities of information, and it may make it challenging for them to retain instructions about social media along with all the other guidance they are receiving. This does not necessarily require re-convening athletes for formal instruction; updates could be sent through social media about news items of relevance, or coaches and administrators could check in with athletes at regular intervals regarding social media experiences.

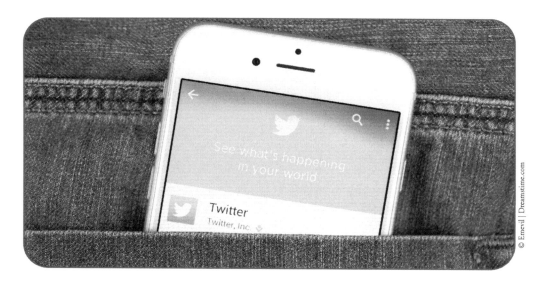

How will the education be presented? Will someone within the organization provide the training or will an outside speaker be brought in? Utilizing someone within the organization can provide familiarity and credibility with athletes, yet that familiarity also can prompt them to tune out; therefore, a fresh voice may help increase attention and participation. Will the education consist of traditional lecture format, or will it be more informal and encourage participation and engagement from the audience? It may be difficult to conduct training in small groups, given the constraints on athletes' schedules. In general, however, presenting in small groups can be more conducive to participation and interaction. If this is not feasible or practical, periodic follow-up can help achieve these same outcomes.

Will education involve examples from athletes, or will outside examples be used? This can be a sensitive topic. On one hand, using examples of social media posts from athletes in the organization can enhance the relevance and applicability of the training with athletes. Yet, on the other hand, it also could cause resentment as an athlete may feel as though he/she is being "called out" in front of his/her peers. In these situations, it is advisable to let the athlete know beforehand that his/her example is going to be used in the training, or at a minimum, make sure that both positive and negative examples from the same athlete are used. According to social cognitive theory (Bandura, 1977, 2001), people learn behaviors from seeing mediated examples and tend to disregard responses that cause unrewarding effects. With respect to social media education, athletes who see positive examples and see other athletes being rewarded for positive social media use are, theoretically, more likely to adopt positive behaviors than if they are exposed solely to negative examples.

How will the education be assessed? Just as the social media plan as a whole needs to be assessed and modified on a consistent basis, so too should athlete education. This can be done through simple survey measures or by monitoring the number of problematic incidents between training sessions. In research conducted by Sanderson, Browning, and Schmittel (2015) with a sample of Division I student-athletes, they discovered that student-athletes had difficulty recalling any memorable messages about social media education. While these results may be unique to the student-athletes they interviewed, these results suggest that following up and evaluating social media education efforts may help ensure that athletes retain and implement the information presented to them during social media training.

Will athletes be given a social media policy? Policies can be helpful because they provide athletes with boundaries for behavior and set guidelines for what the organization considers to be acceptable and unacceptable social media behavior. There are several important factors that should be considered in social media policies:

- **Who will write the policy?** Certainly someone with responsibility for the overall social media plan can be tasked with writing the policy, but to protect the organization it would be prudent to do this in consultation with Human Resources personnel or legal counsel. Additionally, an outside consultant can be used to develop a policy, which may be worth the investment to allow organization employees to focus efforts into other areas. It may also be beneficial to bring in athletes, as well as other stakeholder groups (e.g., those involved with student-athlete welfare, high school principals, high school parents), when crafting a policy. This can help ensure buy-in, because the athletes have a voice at the table and are involved in participative governance.

- **Will the policy be specific or vague?** There is great variation in social media polices in this respect. Some organizations use ambiguous language such as "inappropriate" whereas others define what "inappropriate" means. Sanderson and Browning (2013) interviewed student-athletes about messages they received about Twitter and found that most athletes were simply told not to do anything "stupid" but were not provided with clear and specific direction about what that term meant. While it may seem unnecessary to explain such terms, it is important to remember that there are generational differences about what is considered inappropriate. Educational sessions can certainly be used to expound on terms used in the policy, but how this will play out in the policy is an important facet to consider.

- **Will both positive and negative examples be utilized?** Sanderson (2011b) analyzed social media policies from Division I athletic programs and found that the vast majority of the policies only talked about the negative uses of social media, with very little discussion on how social media could be used in beneficial ways. As noted earlier, given how prominent social media is in the lives of most athletes, particularly those who are younger, it is not realistic to expect them to give up using social media. Thus, how can athletes be taught to maximize the potential social media offers to build a personal brand, build professional networks, and promote their accomplishments?

  As one example, Clemson University baseball pitcher Matthew Crownover used Twitter to report on his experiences attending the Society for American Baseball Research (SABR) Conference.

As noted earlier, positively reinforcing athletes who use social media in commendable ways may be an effective way to teach athletes how to use social media responsibly. Using an example like this may do much more for policy effectiveness than simply listing nothing but restrictions.

- **Will the policy outline consequences?** Some social media policies are vague about discipline, while others are very specific. While not providing specific information can provide the organization with more latitude in handling cases, it also may prompt athletes to think that nothing significant will happen for violating a policy. Although providing definitive action steps might limit the organization's ability to discipline, it may resonate more receptively with athletes. One way to compensate for this limitation is to use the phrase "up to and including" to provide latitude to issue more severe discipline for more problematic incidents. Additionally, a statement in the policy that indicates that the organization "reserves the right to assess each violation on an individual basis" also can provide more flexibility in handling cases.
- **Will the policy be signed?** One of the challenges an organization faces is proving that an employee was informed of a policy. Having athletes sign the policy, while

burdensome, provides much more protection in the event that an athlete wishes to challenge discipline. This is more likely to be relevant to amateur athletics; in professional sports, this issue may be covered under a collective bargaining agreement.

While the above topics are major components of a social media policy, there are several other factors that also should be considered:

How will the organization promote positive social media usage by athletes? In the examples provided earlier, the University of Washington featured student-athletes' social media content on their website, and in the example with Matthew Crownover, the Clemson Athletics Department reported on his trip to the SABR conference, featuring a blog he wrote about his experiences on the athletic department website. Athletes have lots of positive experiences to share, and featuring these actions builds goodwill with fans and other stakeholders and portrays the organization in a positive light. Relying on the media to cover positive stories is a tenuous proposition at best, so social media should be used to tell positive stories associated with the organization.

How will the organization respond when a misstep occurs? There are a variety of image repair and crisis communication strategies that can be called upon when issues occur. These range from denying the incident, to shifting the blame, to accepting responsibility for the incident and outlining a plan of corrective action (Benoit, 1995). For a sport organization, deciding *ahead* of time how these incidents will be handled will increase the effectiveness of the response—and given how closely the media covers social media missteps, a response will have to be provided. In general, the more an organization or athlete addresses the issue and outlines steps being taken to prevent future occurrences, the more satisfactory the result with the public (Sanderson & Emmons, 2014). Accordingly, it will be more beneficial in the long run, even if difficult in the short run, to address the issue head on.

In summary, athletes will continue to be major players on social media platforms, and to some degree, their presence accounts for social media's popularity. Fans now have unique opportunities to access and engage athletes, and athletes have the ability to take more control of their public portrayals. Nevertheless, there also are potential pitfalls, and it is important that social media plans contain a component governing how athletes' social media usage will be managed and how social media education will occur.

Consider sharing these 10 tips with athletes on positive, effective, and appropriate social media use. Although directed towards student-athletes, the list is a good reminder for athletes at all levels.

10 SOCIAL MEDIA TIPS FOR STUDENT-ATHLETES

1. Every day is a job interview.
2. Twitter/social media is a live 24/7 press conference that never turns off.
3. Take pride in who/what you represent.

4. If you can't say it in front of your mother, then don't say it.
5. Use common sense. Think: if I hit send, will I get in trouble? Before you hit send, wait 10 seconds.
6. Don't engage in Twitter arguments. No one wins.
7. What happens behind closed doors . . . stays behind closed doors.
8. Thank your teammates and fans every day.
9. Never criticize an opposing team, referee, coach, or teammate.
10. Have fun.

CHAPTER QUESTIONS

You work for a sport organization and a coach asks you if the players should be restricted from using social media during the season. What do you recommend and why?

_____
_____
_____
_____
_____
_____
_____
_____

What factors should be considered in crafting a social media education plan for athletes?

_____
_____
_____
_____
_____
_____
_____
_____

What factors should be considered in crafting a social media policy?

_____
_____
_____
_____

_____

_____

_____

_____

_____

Conduct an internet search for a social media policy for athletes (it will be helpful to search for policies used in intercollegiate athletics). Analyze the policy and identify strengths and weaknesses.

_____

_____

_____

_____

_____

_____

_____

_____

Is it important to emphasize positive social media examples along with negative examples? Why or why not?

_____

_____

_____

_____

_____

_____

_____

Why would including athletes in social media plans, education, and policies be productive for the organization?

_____

_____

_____

_____

_____

_____

_____

_____

You work for a sport organization and one of the athletes just posted something controversial that made national news headlines. How would you respond?

_____

_____

_____

_____

_____

_____

_____

_____

_____

INDUSTRY INTERVIEW

Kevin DeShazo, President and Founder
Fieldhouse Media

Should an athlete's social media content be integrated into a sport organization's social media plan? Why or why not?

For professional organizations, it would make sense to integrate the social media content of their players into the overall social media plan, but there are challenges with that. Many times, depending on the league, the collective bargaining agreement (CBA) impacts what organizations can and can't do regarding athletes on social media.

Organizations would love to leverage the presence of their athletes, but many times athletes are more interested (and obligated) to meet the needs of their sponsors. This results in many professional organizations being surprisingly hands-off when it comes to athletes on social media.

That said, it would be beneficial for organizations to leverage the power and followings of their players. The power in social media is for the individual vs. the organization (in or out of sports), so finding ways to incorporate the athletes and their content into the overall strategy for the organization is a must.

In what ways can athletes pursue individual social media goals and organizational social media goals?

In some respect, the goals for the athletes will align with that of the organization. They both want loyal, engaged followings who show up not only on game day but also are active consumers of the brand's products. They both want to (or should want to) build relationships that matter with their fan base, an army of supporters, and advocates. So when athletes are promoting not only themselves but also the organization (and their teammates) as a whole, it is a win for both. Fans are not just fans of an athlete or just fans of an organization, they are fans of both. So the more you can hit on their loyalty to both, it increases the benefit. Sports are a team effort. It should be the same on social media.

Should athletes be more authentic or scripted on social media?

There is a time and a place for both, but I tend to think there is more power and benefit in authenticity. Fans see through sponsored, scripted content and are turned off by cheesy motivational quotes. They follow athletes to know who they really are. It is powerful when athletes give fans access into who they are and what they are about. That said, athletes don't have to show the *whole* version of themselves. They can and should tweet about more than just sports, but should be guarded with opinions on sensitive or controversial topics (as all individuals should). Fans don't want to see scripted, brand-type tweets all day and they don't want to see a bunch of profanity and locker-room talk. There's a healthy balance that athletes can find, which is where they can truly build a powerful, valuable community.

What social media platforms hold the most utility for athletes?

It really depends on the athlete and what their goals are. Twitter seemed to take over for the past two years but we're seeing Facebook make a comeback, specifically with longer announcements like Landon Donovan's retirement. Instagram has exploded as well for athletes as a way to truly give an inside look into their lives. When they don't have words to share/tweet, they can simply post a picture. Some have noted that they feel they can be a little more laid back on Instagram, a little more real.

At the end of the day, I think it is where they can most effectively reach their fans and have real engagement with them. In my mind, as it stands in mid- to late-2014, that platform is still Twitter. From sending a message to the masses in real-time to communicating one on one via @replies or direct messages, Twitter makes that almost effortless.

Should social media education for athletes be part of an organization's social media plan? Why or why not?

Education is an absolute must when it comes to athletes representing an organization. Everything they do online reflects on the organization and they need to understand that responsibility. They are out to build their own brand, which is certainly understandable, but there is more at stake. Most of this education—and to call it that is a stretch—is handled by agents or marketing firms that a given athlete works with. Rarely is it something that the actual organization facilitates, so we are sending multi-million (billion?) dollar assets out into the world to represent us without preparing them for that setting. Again, with some CBAs there can be issues, but discussing social media with athletes, from an organizational perspective, is crucial.

INTERVIEW QUESTIONS

Kevin DeShazo indicated that it would be beneficial for sport organizations to leverage the social media audiences of athletes into their social media plans. How might they do this?

_____

_____

_____

_____

_____

_____

_____

How can sport organizations use social media to capitalize on the loyalty fans have to both the team and the athletes?

_____
_____
_____
_____
_____
_____
_____
_____

DeShazo suggested that Twitter is the most viable platform for athletes to most effectively reach fans and engage with them. Do you agree? Why or why not?

_____
_____
_____
_____
_____
_____
_____
_____

DeShazo suggested that it is more optimal for athletes to be genuine when using social media. How can an organization encourage this while at the same time reducing risk of incident?

_____
_____
_____
_____
_____
_____
_____

5

Social Media Issues and Challenges

Sport organizations face unique challenges on social media. For instance, organization personnel must decide how to address employee use and how to react to criticisms on social media. Consequently, there have been a number of policy and legal issues that have arisen. Some of these include the following:

- **Organizations screening job candidates by accessing their social media accounts.** In some cases, this includes requesting that applicants provide usernames and passwords. Sport organizations are increasingly using social media to screen athletes both at the professional and amateur levels.

- **Organizations monitoring social media usage by employees and disciplining employees for social media content.** This includes termination of employment. It is important to note here that the loss of ownership over content plays a pertinent role here. Once a person shares a message on a social media platform, they lose control over that message and what can be done with it. A vivid example involved a nurse who was suspended for a Facebook post relating to a shooting in Washington, D. C. One of her Facebook friends, who also was a co-worker, took

a screen shot of the post and turned it in to company management (Carman, 2013). Thus, even if an athlete or an employee of a sport organization has a private account, there is nothing preventing anyone who has access to that account from capturing the content in a similar manner.

- **Organizations utilizing social media at inopportune times.** One example in this respect involves the Baltimore Ravens' team Twitter account. The Ravens live-tweeted former player Ray Rice's press conference that was being held for him to respond to an assault allegation against his then fiancé. Given the gravity of the situation, Rice used what can be considered a poor word choice, "Failure is not getting knocked down. It's not getting up," which the team account tweeted verbatim. This resulted in people commenting about what they perceived to be a lack of sensitivity towards the issue and criticism from several sport media outlets (Yoder, 2014). Clearly, it was not the Ravens' intent to undermine the seriousness of the issue, but that was a perception that was expressed by some columnists and Twitter users.

Sometimes even the best of intentions can bring unexpected—and unwanted—results. It is important to note that social media plans include a component on how to deal with sensitive situations and to what extent to mention/include players in social media who have been involved in legal or other off-the-field issues. One example in this respect involves Florida State University quarterback Jameis Winston. On August 10, 2014, the Florida State football Twitter account began a sort of forum on Twitter for fans to ask Jameis Winston questions accompanied by the hashtag #AskJameis.

Again, while making athletes available to answer questions via social media is generally a great way to engage fans, in this case, considering that Winston had been involved in several incidents away from the playing field, the hashtag was "hijacked." Essentially the hashtag was transformed into a way for people to mock Winston and the Florida State program, rather than being an avenue to field questions from fans (Newell, 2014). It may be in the best interest of all involved to avoid making an athlete available to answer questions from fans on social media who has experienced legal or other private issues, even if that athlete has considerable star power.

Earlier, we talked about some of the issues that have arisen within organizations with social media. At the core, these issues are centered on privacy. Thus, it makes sense to question the extent of privacy on social media. While the case law pertaining to social media is still being sorted out, and indeed is continually shifting, in general there is not a reasonable expectation to privacy on social media. This occurs for several reasons:

- **One of the main determinations in concluding if there is a reasonable expectation of privacy centers on if a person "knowingly" exposed something to another person, or to the public at large.** In the context of social media, even though a person may have a private account, even if she/he has just one follower/friend, she/he has voluntarily exposed something to another person by sharing a post. Additionally, if the person has a public account that does not utilize any privacy settings, she/he has arguably exposed information to the public at large as well. Moreover, even though there may be times when a person regrets posting a social media message, it is difficult to prove ignorance. That fact that a person has to log on to a site, type a message, and hit send suggests that she/he is knowingly revealing something.

- **Social media is predicated on sharing.** Think back to the first chapter and the qualities that make something "social media": *sharing, collaboration,* and *community.* It is difficult to presume that someone is using social media to be secretive when those qualities underpin the whole experience. One judge, in ruling that Facebook was not private, indicated, "Only the uninitiated or foolish could believe that Facebook is an online box of secrets" (Present, 2013). Swapping out any other social media platform for Facebook would be unlikely to change legal minds.

  With this foundation in place, what are some of the issues facing sport organizations when it comes to social media and privacy? We offer several below:

© Lilja | Dreamstime.com

- **Disciplining employees for social media content.** While it is easy to default to athletes, a sport organization is comprised of a host of other employees who use social media. For example, in 2009, the Philadelphia Eagles fired a gameday employee for a Facebook post that was critical of the team's decision not to re-sign veteran player Brian Dawkins (Florio, 2009). It is also important to note here that discipline is very dependent on the type of sport organization. For professional sport organizations, athletes are in most cases unionized, and so any action taken for social media content would have to factor that agreement into consideration. For any other employee group that might happen to be unionized, the same considerations would apply. At amateur levels, discipline may largely center on the extent to which NCAA violations are involved. Former University of North Carolina football player Marvin Austin provides an illustrative example. Prior to the 2010 season, Austin was dismissed for receiving improper benefits, thereby violating the NCAA's ethical conduct rules. The investigation came about because of his Twitter messages (Hauer, 2013).

Specifically, Austin was tweeting about how he was tired of not having money, and provided images documenting expensive products. His tweets garnered media attention and ultimately led to the NCAA investigation (Hauer, 2013).

- **Restricting social media usage.** As discussed earlier, one strategy that is adopted with athletes is restricting their social media usage. This topic, along with that of disciplining athletes for social media content, raises the question of free speech. This is a logical issue to arise. With respect to discipline, in most cases, a person is not protected from consequences of his/her speech on social media. Again, a person has a right to say whatever she/he wants to on social media, but a private organization has every right to discipline a person for that speech. It really is no different than if a person was to utter a threat in person to his/her boss. Yes, the person has the right to say such a thing, but the organization also has a right to terminate employment for that behavior.

  With respect to restricting social media usage, a key term that comes in to play here is Time, Place, and Manner (TPM) restrictions. Based on TPM, an organization can regulate speech (thus the TPM restrictions) so long as there is an opportunity to communicate in alternative ways. For instance, a head coach could restrict social media from being used during the season, but could not restrict communication entirely. Thus, if a coach were to ban both social media and face-to-face communication, there would be an issue. However, as coaches only restrict social media, but allow other types of communication, there is less legal liability. One interesting thing to note here is that in general, there has been little done in the way of holding fans accountable for hateful messages sent to athletes, although this may be changing. One fan was arrested in October 2013 for sending threatening messages via Twitter to several New York Mets players and the organization (Ackert, 2013). Similarly, in 2012, a teenager was arrested in England for sending out threatening messages to British diver Tom Daley (Dodds, 2012).

- **Monitoring social media content.** Within recent years, there has emerged a cottage industry of social media monitoring services. The providers of these services utilize a variety of methods to monitor athletes' content, some of which has come under criticism (Dickey, 2012). While monitoring can be useful, it is important for sport organization personnel tasked with social media plans to determine if they will monitor athletes' private messages, public messages, or both. If private messages are going to be monitored, it is important to be aware of state laws, as in some states (approximately 10), it is illegal to require students or job applicants to provide social media passwords. Additionally, monitoring should not be viewed as a substitute for education. Sanderson and Browning (2013) argued that educating athletes about social media on the front end would make monitoring on the back end less necessary.

  There may also be resistance among athletes if private accounts are going to be monitored, as athletes may perceive these to be off limits. An optimal solution may be to monitor only public messages, and to combine monitoring with education (i.e., understanding what the issues are and focusing educational efforts on those topics).

- **Hateful messages.** Although this is not something a sport organization is necessarily responsible for, given the nature of some of the vitriolic messages sent to athletes via social media, it is important that sport organizations have a plan in place to help athletes deal with this issue. Education can be helpful here, by simply letting athletes know that this behavior is unacceptable and that the organization will support them in dealing with it. For example, Browning and Sanderson (2012) interviewed student-athletes about getting criticized on Twitter, and found that while there were differences in how the athletes reacted to these messages, there was a consistent theme of being angry and upset by them. Since athletes have spent years developing their skills and talents, it should not be surprising that they would experience these feelings. Indeed, there are very few people who "like" criticism. Thanks to social media, every one of us has the ability to have things said about us, and it is a natural human reaction to want to know what those things are. The challenge with respect to hateful messages is working with athletes to ensure that they feel safe and providing appropriate resources to help prevent any mental health issues.

  It also is important, particularly for younger athletes, to be aware of the mental health and psychological issues that might result from being the recipient of these kinds of messages. Sanderson and Truax (2014) investigated hateful messages sent via Twitter to University of Alabama kicker Cade Foster after the team lost to Auburn University in November 2013. These messages contained threatening and demeaning commentary such as:

  > "@Foster_43 when I find you on campus I'm gonna show you how to kick—with a swift one to the nuts. Jackass, thought u would learn after LSU" (p. 340).

  > "@Foster_43 Wow thanks for making us lose, everybody hates you now" (p. 340).

  > "@Foster_43 hey kill yourself. Seriously. Do it." (p. 342)

  There also were extremely offensive and vulgar comments that suggested Foster and his mother should be sexually violated. Whereas some athletes might be unaffected by these messages, it is not difficult to imagine how they could cause an athlete psychological harm—not only when receiving them personally but also when a family member is the target of these messages, as in the case of Steve Blake mentioned earlier in the text.

While this chapter has discussed several of the legal and policy challenges associated with social media, there will surely be many more that manifest as social media continues to advance. One emerging area to monitor is Google Glass and other types of wearable technology. While such devices have great utility to provide insider or "birds-eye" points of view for fans, they also introduce monitoring issues of which sport organizations may need to be wary. An athlete could easily find him/herself in a situation of being recorded without knowledge. Additionally, there have been several incidents where college coaches have been suspended or terminated due to audio recordings of verbal aggressiveness being released to the public and wearable technology could be another way to "out" this behavior.

Although it can be daunting to keep up with all the social media trends and adapt the social media plan accordingly, there are a number of resources to assist in this endeavor. First, there are a large number of individuals who work in sport and social media who routinely share information and best practices with each other (as Kirby Garry noted in his interview in an earlier chapter). There are a variety of Twitter chats held at dedicated times devoted to various aspects of sport social media. No one person can really be an expert on social media—it changes too quickly. However, there is a wealth of collective intelligence available that helps promote the common objectives those working in sport and social media are chasing. Second, there is a growing body of academic research that is devoted to sport and social media, and this work can be of great value to those responsible for creating, administering, and modifying an organization's social media plan. Many academic researchers are willing to work with industry practitioners, and collaborations between industry and academia should be pursued with more vigor. Third, there are a growing number of panels and presentations related to sport and social media at professional association meetings and conferences. These events provide both the opportunity to learn and the ability to foster networking among all types of individuals involved in social media.

In summary, social media provides a wealth of advantages, but those opportunities come with a variety of diverse challenges as well. Sport organization personnel tasked with social media plans need to invest in education and resources to ensure that the social media plan remains compliant with changing legal views, and keeps pace with technological evolution.

CHAPTER QUESTIONS

Should sport organization personnel use social media to evaluate athletes they are considering bringing into the organization? Why or why not?

If you worked for a sport organization, and you were asked for a recommendation about monitoring athletes' social media messages, how would you respond?

_____

_____

_____

_____

_____

_____

_____

_____

Conduct research on vendors who provide social media monitoring for sport organizations. Select two providers and compare the services they provide and the methods they use to perform the service. Then make a recommendation on which vendor you would hire.

_____

_____

_____

_____

_____

_____

_____

_____

Is it reasonable for athletes or key figures in sport organizations to expect privacy on social media? Why or why not?

_____

_____

_____

_____

_____

_____

_____

_____

If you worked in a sport organization and were tasked with helping athletes deal with hateful messages received via social media, how you go about it?

_____

_____

_____

_____

_____

_____

_____

_____

Conduct research and look for incidents where fans have sent hateful messages to athletes on social media. Share some of the messages with your peers and discuss how sport organizations can address this issue. Ask, "Is it possible to remedy this issue?"

_____

_____

_____

_____

_____

_____

_____

_____

INDUSTRY INTERVIEWS

Michael McCann, Professor and Director, University of New Hampshire Sports & Entertainment Law Institute, Legal Analyst—Sports Illustrated, SI.com & NBATV

Do organizations have any legal risk/liability with social media content? If so, what does that risk look like?

Yes, there is risk that social media content could be defamatory. There is also risk that privacy rights are infringed if confidential information is shared on social media without the appropriate consent.

Do sport organizations that restrict/monitor athletes' social media content open themselves up to legal liability? Why or why not?

Yes, sport organizations that restrict or monitor athletes' social media are essentially acting as a gatekeeper and therefore are more implicated should the athlete be able to make a statement through social media that has negative legal consequences.

If an employee puts a disclaimer on his/her social media account indicating that content does not reflect the views of the team, does that really act as a safeguard from consequences? Why or why not?

I think a disclaimer helps, but there is nothing to stop a journalist from saying that a person who works for a team made a particular statement on social media. A disclaimer only separates the team from the statement, but not from the person who made the statement and their relationship to the team.

Are there legal risks in using social media content to evaluate athletes, whether that is at the collegiate or professional level?

Probably not, unless the information is confidential.

INTERVIEW QUESTIONS

What kinds of confidential information could a sport organization share on social media that might expose it to liability?

_____

_____

_____

_____

_____

_____

_____

_____

Is it a good idea for a sport organization to act as a gatekeeper? Why or why not?

_____

_____

_____

_____

_____

_____

_____

Michael McCann suggested that a disclaimer on social media does not separate a person from their relationship to the team. Do you agree? Why or why not?

_____

_____

_____

_____

_____

_____

_____

Although McCann indicated that there are no legal risks to using social media to evaluate athletes unless confidential information is being considered, is that a good practice? Why or why not?

_____

_____

_____

_____

_____

_____

_____

6

Implementing and Managing the Plan

Once the plan has been formulated, the next challenge is executing and overseeing it. This may go without saying, but it is important that the plan be documented (written) not only so there is something to reference, but also to ensure that those who have responsibility for various components of the plan have a guide to follow and can be held accountable. This will require a collective effort within the organization. The plan has to be embedded into every segment/operational area of the organization. As we noted earlier, one of the decisions a sport organization will have to make is the number of voices the organization will have on social media. It is important that—even though some employees may not have direct responsibility for social media content—each employee be made aware of the social media plan and be encouraged to contact the appropriate person if she/he is aware of something that may be of value to share on social media. It is very unlikely that the person/team running a social media account (especially those running the principle account) can be aware of every bit of news happening within the organization.

© Chagin | Dreamstime.com

Accordingly, communicating the plan to each employee (perhaps posting it on a specific place on the company intranet) and letting people know that they can submit ideas will help get buy-in from the organization collectively, and help employees feel invested in the plan. While this doesn't mean that every suggestion has to be implemented, it is still important to thank the employee for his/her suggestion and provide a brief rationale for why the item may not be included (e.g., "Thanks for the suggestion; unfortunately we have some other stories we plan to run right now, but this might be something we would revisit down the road"). We mentioned earlier that social media enables sport organizations to tell their stories, and fostering this inclusivity with all employees is a valuable way to make sure all the stories worth telling get discovered and promoted.

In developing a social media plan, there are certain goals and objectives to be achieved and there are various ways to meet them. An essential task is identifying who will be responsible for the various parts of the plan. Once these individuals are identified, it is important that individual meetings be held where workloads and other obligations can be discussed, and then the expectations of social media content and management can be reviewed. For example, how often is the person expected to post and what should be the ratio of posts (e.g., informative vs. personal interest vs. humorous)? Staffing contingencies are another important aspect of the plan: What will happen if the employee is pulled into other duties and is not able to run the account for a period of time? What if the employee is out sick? While social media can be run from any location with an Internet connection, it will be important to assess the resource needs and how exigencies will be handled. Social media is a time commitment; there is significant planning that goes into determining the content of posts. The actual posting of the content is just a small fraction of the overall social media plan. An editorial calendar can be an excellent tool that provides a visual view of what days content will be posted and how much content is to be posted (Folger, n.d.b).

Many content management platforms (e.g., Hootsuite) enable posts to be scheduled, which aids in efficiency. A word of caution here: While this can be helpful (e.g., game times are known well in advance) it is important to adjust scheduled posts if events require it. For example, if there is a national tragedy or sensitive story getting a lot of media traction, it is wise to cancel scheduled postings until the story has passed. The subject of sensitive issues within social media should be discussed, with the goal of understanding to what extent social media will be altered by bad news. Will employees be expected to refrain from commenting on these issues? What is the process that is to be followed with critical comments received via social media? Does the employee have the ability to respond to the critic, or will this be elevated to another person in the organization? One approach to such a situation is to directly respond to those who are making these statements. One interesting example in this respect occurred with University of Mississippi Athletic Director Ross Bjork. On December 31, 2014, after Mississippi lost the Peach Bowl against Texas Christian University, Mississippi quarterback Bo Wallace received critical comments on Twitter for his performance. In particular, one cartoonist made a comment that Bjork responded to. Different people then began weighing in both supporting and criticizing Bjork for his actions. Bjork's final tweet called for a truce, stating that he respects the cartoonist, but will always stand up for his team. Certainly, this strategy might not work for or be appropriate for every sport organization, but it does present a compelling case study in sport administrators taking to Twitter to defend organization members.

Another important part of implementing the plan centers on engagement. To what extent will interaction take place with fans? Remember that interaction does not always mean having a conversation or answering every question or mention. Certainly, there should be times where messages are acknowledged and questions are answered, but engagement can merely be asking a question (e.g., "Alright fans, who is going to be the player of the game tonight?") to which unique and compelling responses can easily be re-tweeted. While every organization has different resource levels, in general social media strategy should follow the 80/20 principle, where 80% of activity is "being friendly" through re-tweets, engagement, and other forms of interaction, whereas the 20% is the ability to add new content (Folger, n. d.a). This concept aligns with the ability to optimize the power of social media, which comes through building and developing relationships.

Implementing and managing the plan also requires "listening." In other words, in addition to posting content, there has to be effort expended to see what is being said about the organization across various social networks. In addition to searching for the name of the organization, this also should involve searching for names of athletes and coaches or any other pertinent information relevant to the organization, including hashtags. Remember that social media is a channel for feedback, and while the feedback and perceptions being expressed may be inaccurate, they nonetheless represent what a certain segment of individuals think about the organization. Sport organizations can classify this kind of information hierarchically and develop response plans based on where the feedback falls in that classification. For example, if a fan mentions the organization on Twitter complaining about the team losing a game, responding is likely to be ineffective and may actually enflame the situation. However, if a fan mentions the organization account on Twitter to complain about a bad-service experience at the game, that is an opportunity to reach out, assess the situation, and, if warranted, make it right and cultivate the perception that the organization genuinely cares about the fan experience.

A final issue to consider with implementation centers on finances. An organization must consider the fiscal resources it can invest in social media. This involves not only salaries of those who have direct responsibility, but also involves peripheral needs, such as computer programs (e.g., do we have a program that allows us to put out high quality infographics?) and video equipment. While text will always have currency in social media, there is a sizable shift occurring with visual content, and accordingly, there is no room for choppy video or blurred pictures. Having high-quality social media posts reflects on the quality of the organization.

Clearly, organizations have differing levels of resources, and this all has to be incorporated into the design and implementation of a plan. A Division III athletic department may not be able to do everything on social media that an NFL team can do, nor should they try to, as the audiences for those two organizations are different and have different needs and desires. While organizations can learn from one another, it is important to stay true to the culture and values that make each organization unique.

CHAPTER QUESTIONS

How can a sport organization help all its employees become invested in the social media plan?

_____

_____

_____

_____

_____

_____

_____

_____

_____

Why should sport organizations listen to what is being said about them on social media?

_____

_____

_____

_____

_____

_____

_____

_____

How should sport organizations respond to criticism on social media? Are there certain criticisms that should be ignored? Why or why not?

_____

_____

_____

_____

_____

_____

_____

_____

_____

If you were responsible for overseeing a social media plan that had multiple people running accounts, would you empower them to respond to criticism? Why or why not?

_____

_____

_____

_____

_____

_____

_____

_____

If you were advising a professional sports team on social media, how many posts would you recommend they make each day? How would this be different if you were advising an intercollegiate athletics department?

_____

_____

_____

_____

_____

_____

_____

_____

Do you agree with the 80/20 rule for social media content? Why or why not?

_____

_____

_____

_____

_____

_____

_____

_____

_____

Reflect on the example in the chapter of Mississippi Athletic Director Ross Bjork defending players on Twitter. Is this a good strategy for an athletic director or sport organization administrator? Why or why not? Additionally, what variables might determine whether this is a good strategy to employ for a sport organization?

_____

_____

_____

_____

_____

_____

_____

_____

_____

INDUSTRY INTERVIEW

Eric Nichols, Associate Athletic Director/Marketing, University of South Carolina

How important is it to get buy-in from organization leaders for a social media plan?

Getting buy-in is vital to reach the true potential of a department or team. However, buy-in is not mandatory for success in the social space. At South Carolina we view our current strategy with our social media plan a success as we have been able to accomplish our goals of communicating our key messages directly to our fans as well as engaging in one-to-one conversations even though we have barriers to success at key leadership positions.

What kind of resources (both employee and financial) should be devoted to a social media plan?

While social media plans are not a one-person operation, I strongly believe that there needs to be at least one person within an organization that can remain the expert on the tools as well as championing the integration and education efforts. The social media leader can either be a stand-alone position, a department of multiple individuals, or someone who also has other responsibilities. Financially, the resources need to be made available to accommodate the previously mentioned expectations. Beyond the personnel, there are only minimal hardware costs and measurement software needed.

How important is feedback and evaluation in managing a social media plan?

All plans, whether they be social media or otherwise, require a scoreboard of some sort. (How would you know if you are winning?!) Due to its fluid nature, regular evaluation is necessary in social media to maintain best practices for accomplishing your goals. Unfortunately, not only do new tools emerge, but existing tools also change their platform on a regular basis. At South Carolina, feedback is at the heart of our social media strategy. We use the acronym SEAL (Source, Engage, Amplify, and Listen) to guide our team and tactics, and the feedback we receive by regularly listening to our fans is a significant advantage in shaping our message.

At what point should a social media plan change? Is it important to be flexible? Why or why not?

A social media plan should be nimble enough to be tweaked for emerging tools and strategies, but the core purpose for using the tools shouldn't be altered too frequently. Social media is an immediate petri dish where new tactics and ideas emerge on a regular basis and your plan shouldn't be so rigid as to not be able to adjust to a new idea. Sometimes a plan needs to change due to an adjustment made by a tool, like when Facebook began changing their algorithm. Several years ago we would post game updates to Facebook, but when Facebook started penalizing content that was not engaging and rewarding posts with media, our plan needed to be changed.

INTERVIEW QUESTIONS

Eric Nichols suggested that buy-in is not mandatory for success in the social space. Do you agree? Why or why not?

_____

_____

_____

_____

_____

_____

_____

_____

Nichols uses the term SEAL to guide the South Carolina social media team. What acronyms can you come up with to measure social media effectiveness for a sport organization?

_____

_____

_____

_____

_____

_____

_____

Nichols indicates that feedback is at the core of South Carolina's social media strategy. Do you think that's a good anchor for social media strategy? Why or why not?

_____

_____

_____

_____

_____

_____

_____

Is it important for social media practitioners in sport to be aware of changes that social media platforms make to their site (such as changing algorithms)? Why or why not?

_____
_____
_____
_____
_____
_____
_____
_____

7

Measuring the Success of the Plan

O nce a social media plan has been created and implemented within a sport organization, it requires consistent evaluation. In fact, given how fast social media changes, there will likely be a frequent need to evaluate and modify the social media plan. There are some important questions to ask here, which include:

- How does the organization know it is "winning" on social media? And more importantly, what counts as a "win?" If the organization is not winning consistently, what needs to change?
- How are social media messages being received? Are the messages getting traction with fans and other stakeholders? If not, why not? And what needs to be done differently?
- Is the organization listening to the feedback being received via social media? What is being done with this information?

Another reason to measure the success of the plan is that it helps emphasize the value of social media to decision-makers and executives. Talk to anyone who works in sport and social media and she/he has probably heard this question over and over: "What is the

return on investment (ROI) of social media?" The repetition of this question under-scores its significance, and by developing a strategic social media plan and continually monitoring and modifying it, it can clearly be answered. Further, the ROI of social media can be effectively demonstrated by these factors:

- **Goals.** Reporting that the team account had 15 Twitter updates and 10 Facebook posts does not demonstrate ROI, because it will be followed with "So what?" So, if one of the organization's goals is to increase in-game attendance, how can social media be used to do that? One potential answer is to encourage fans to share content while at games; for unique and compelling posts, reward fans by acknowledging their message, and perhaps even offering the fan merchandise or concessions as an additional reward. Thus, a social media report should consist of, "Our tweet about the game-winning shot was re-tweeted 1,000 times, the Instagram hashtag we promoted for the game was used 3,500 times, and our concession hashtag resulted in $2,500 in sales during the game last night." There are now technological advancements to help in this area. For example, software programs that enable social media content to be searched within geographic proximity are now available, and this kind of capability can allow an organization to see how many people are talking about the organization at (or very near) its location and to then take action and respond to those messages.

  As another example, if an organization's goal is reach or visibility, how can social media assist in meeting this objective? For instance, a sport organization could create a hashtag that could be promoted on billboards and other traditional forms of advertising to encourage social conversations about an upcoming game. Additionally, creative videos or other storytelling features could be created to generate traffic and "buzz" around the organization. As one example, the Clemson University Athletic Communications staff created a video segment where quarterback Cole Stoudt posed as a mannequin and then jumped out to scare teammates as they entered the football complex. The video was viewed over 1,000,000 times on YouTube.

  Creative content and hashtags can go a long way in driving the visibility of the organization. Additionally, consider the audience size of a sport organization social media account. For instance, if a team has 200,000 followers on Twitter, what is it worth to reach 200,000 people? Using traditional advertising rates and the audience size that those messages reach, figures could be extrapolated to ascertain the value of a social media audience. Clearly, not every person will see the tweet, but neither does every potential audience member see a television or radio advertisement. However, if the content is compelling enough, there is a high likelihood that a significant portion of the audience will see the message as people re-transmit the message to others across various social media platforms. This re-transmission spreads the message all at no cost to the organization, other than the resources that went into creating and disseminating the original message.

- **Platform choice.** It can be easy to get caught up in the hype of some of the new social media platforms and trends, but if those trends and platforms do not have relevance to the organization, it may not be worth devoting resources to them. For example, a sport organization may find that many of its fans and other key stakeholders participate more on established social media platforms such as Facebook and Twitter, and less on Snapchat. Therefore, Snapchat may not be an appropriate place to allocate resources. Additionally, some social media platforms have certain characteristics associated with them, and it may be that the image that particular platform carries is not in line with how the organization wishes to be perceived. Some sport organizations may have an identity as "flashy" and "trend-setting" and therefore strive to be quite overt and demonstrative in their social media use. Others, however, may embrace a more traditional culture and therefore maintain a conservative approach to their social media use. In these cases, there is greater risk and less opportunity for return from investing in these platforms or using them in ways that are incongruent with organizational culture. Additionally, does the organization want to be seen as an early adopter or trendsetter? Or, is it more important to cultivate followers on the platforms that the organization already utilizes? In other words, some organizations have an image as being on the leading edge of technology whereas others prefer to sit back and see how others use the platform and work through its nuances before jumping aboard. Still others may find that they are serving the needs of fans and relevant stakeholder groups by using only a select few platforms, while others may perceive that their fans and stakeholders are early adopters; therefore, the organization needs to be at the same place as its fans and stakeholders. Given the importance of being on the relevant social media platforms for an organization's target market, it is very important to understand the preferences and demographics of the target market.

- **Analytical tools.** There are a number of tools and resources that can assist sport organization personnel in evaluating the success of the social media plan. Lepage (n. d.) outlined several useful analytical tools for social media ROI:
  - **Google Analytics**—Google Analytics allows users to track website traffic, conversations that occur on the site, and sign-ups that come from social media campaigns.
  - **Salesforce**—Salesforce provides tracking codes on links that are shared on social media. When packaged with other software, it enables sales to be tracked back to specific social media messages or campaigns.

○ **Hootsuite Analytics**—Hootsuite provides a diverse number of tools that can help track share of voice on social media and which social media platforms are or are not driving traffic to a website.

Within these (and other) tools, reports can be generated that visually depict various social media metrics that provide a snapshot of reach, engagement, and other variables. It is important that these metrics be checked regularly, daily if at all possible.

Finally, one important part of evaluating a social media plan is to be aware of new technological trends. Social media technology is changing constantly, and as it evolves, sport organizations are faced with the challenge of how to react to this information. As noted earlier, this is largely going to be driven by organization culture and resources, but it is important to note that even if new platforms are not being created, users are continually shifting their habits and behaviors on social media sites, and sport organizations need to ensure that they are aware of these changes and modify their messaging on these platforms as needed.

© Andreypopov | Dreamstime.com

CHAPTER QUESTIONS

Why is it important for social media to be tied to organization goals?

_____

_____

_____

_____

_____

_____

_____

_____

_____

How can linking social media to goals help demonstrate social media's ROI?

_____
_____
_____
_____
_____
_____
_____
_____
_____

In what ways is social media valuable for a sport organization?

_____
_____
_____
_____
_____
_____
_____
_____
_____

You work in a sport organization in social media and are asked by a team executive to recommend a social media analytics tool. Conduct research and make a recommendation outlining the benefits and advantages of the tool you select over its competitors.

_____
_____
_____
_____
_____
_____
_____
_____
_____

You work for a sport organization that wants to be on the leading edge of sport and social media. Your supervisor has just ordered Google Glass and asks you to come up with a strategy for using this tool. What strategy do you propose for this wearable technology?

_____

_____

_____

_____

_____

_____

_____

_____

_____

INDUSTRY INTERVIEWS

Alex Restrepo, New Media/Social Media Manager, New Orleans Saints

What kind of ROI variables does your organization use to measure social media success?

Traffic to NewOrleansSaints.com, engagement sponsored posts receive—RTs, Like, Favorite, Clicks to Link (if there is one)—and new followers to the partners account.

Does a social media plan need to impact the bottom line (e.g., ticket sales, concession sales) or can visibility be an indicator of success?

Not every social media plan needs to result in profit to be considered a success. Examples include no-revenue apps like Snapchat and Instagram. We judge the reaction/engagement/press we get from those platforms as signs it was successful. If it helps build/promote your brand and strengthens the relationship with your fans, then that can, in ways, be more valuable than "the bottom line."

How important is it to take risks with a social media plan? Is it okay to have some misses? Why or why not?

It's important to take risks when you want to be ahead of the curve. You have to take risks sometimes in order to be creative. If you just worked on the fence and never pushed the boundaries, that could be boring/predictable, which doesn't get you very far in social media. It's okay to have misses as long as you learn from them. I think every social media team has a campaign or two that didn't go as planned and or they didn't get the level of engagement they were hoping for. That's fine. When working on a social media plan, I try to make three parties happy: front office (ownership/marketing/PR), coaching staff, and fans. If you think all parties would like what that plan represents, it's worth the risk.

Bryan Srabian, Director, Digital Media, San Francisco Giants

What kind of ROI variables does your organization use to measure social media success?

That is the big question, what exactly is the RETURN you are measuring. Increasing ticket sales, retail sales, increased customer service, new sales leads. All are important aspects, and depending on how your organization views social media, some or all of these could be attained. Personally, I feel the overall strategy of your social media is marketing/branding by nature. It becomes the face and voice of your organization. Creating a strong social media content strategy in order to build a highly engaged community is imperative.

Within that, you build value, trust, and have the ability to maximize your results down the road. The ability to sell a sponsorship through social media is maximized with a large and engaged social community. For me, I am measuring engagement/ fan. Are we getting more of our fans to engage with our content? Are they sharing our content, are they responding to it? Are they using our hashtags, conversing with us, about us? I'm measuring the user generated content to see what drives someone to post photos on Instagram of their experience. Was it a promotion or was it organic? All are factors that I measure for our success. My ROI is more focused on ENGAGEMENT than any sales numbers. But I also feel that has a long-term value assessment for the bottom line.

Does a social media plan need to impact the bottom line (e.g., ticket sales, concession sales), or can visibility be an indicator of success?

Everything needs to impact the bottom line. But a social media plan is not always about the short term. Much like it is hard to quantify a billboard or your team's ushers, or a community event. Those are all important factors in their own way, and one can justify that they all have value. But it is hard to quantify their direct impact on the bottom line. I again stress the importance of having that strong engaged community and not really focused on direct sales per se, because I feel that the sales will come as a result when those opportunities present themselves.

Fans continue to purchase more via mobile devices, and social media is part of that, but there is also the fear of turning your social channels into direct sales mediums, and I am very protective of keeping our social channels mostly weighted towards content. I try to keep at least an 80/20 scale of content/marketing for our fans. This way our direct marketing messages can also be positioned as a value proposition without impacting a fan's experience via our social channels.

How important is it to take risks with a social media plan? Is it okay to have some misses? Why or why not?

I think it is important to take risks in all business activity, including and especially social media. Most organizations probably have a social media strategy; what is going to differentiate your strategy from not just other teams, but from media outlets? I feel it is important to innovate, to try new ways of reaching your audience, always measuring the success and tweaking your strategy. You are not going to grow or innovate without taking risks. I feel as long as the risk is not BRAND NEGATIVE (saying or doing something that might damage your brand) the risk is always worth it. My favorite quote is what Wayne Gretzky said. "A good hockey player plays where the puck is. A great hockey player plays where the puck is going to be." And that is what I strive to be, taking risks to go where the puck is going to be.

INTERVIEW QUESTIONS

Alex Restrepo suggested that every social media initiative does not need to result in profit. Do you agree? Why or why not?

_____

_____

_____

_____

_____

_____

_____

Is it worth taking risks to be ahead of the curve when it comes to social media in sport? What factors might determine whether an organization adopts this philosophy regarding social media?

_____

_____

_____

_____

_____

_____

_____

Bryan Srabian indicated he measures social media success by engagement not sales numbers? Is that a good approach? Why or why not?

_____

_____

_____

_____

_____

_____

_____

Chapter Seven

How can a sport organization prevent its social media channels from becoming too sales heavy?

_____

_____

_____

_____

_____

_____

_____

_____

References

300 million: Sharing real moments. (2014, December 10). Retrieved from http://blog.instagram.com/post/104847837897/141210-300million

About Twitter. (n.d.). Retrieved from https://about.twitter.com/company

Ackert, K. (2013, October 24). Threats to the Mets and Citi Field via Twitter get Connecticut man arrested. Retrieved from http://www.nydailynews.com/sports/baseabll/mets/threats-mets-twitter-ct-man-arrested-article-1.1494294

Bandura, A. (1977). *Social learning theory.* Englewood Cliffs, NJ: Prentice Hall.

Bandura, A. (2001). Social cognitive theory of mass communication. *Media Psychology, 3,* 265–299.

Benoit, W. L. (1995). *Accounts, excuses, and apologies: A theory of image restoration strategies.* Albany, NY: State University of New York Press.

Bercovici, J. (2014, June 24). Still more data shows Pinterest passing Twitter in popularity. Retrieved from http://www.forbes.com/sites/jeffbercovici/2014/06/24/still-more-data-shows-pinterest-passing-twitter-in-popularity/

Browning, B., & Sanderson, J. (2012). The positives and negatives of Twitter: Exploring how student-athletes use Twitter and respond to critical tweets. *International Journal of Sport Communication, 5,* 503–521.

Carman, A. (2013, August 26). Fired nurse fails to prove privacy violation regarding Facebook account. Retrieved from http://www.mcknights.com/fired-nurse-fails-to-prove-privacy-violation-regarding-facebook-account/article/308705/

Dickey, J. (2012, May 24). Don't say "Colt 45" or "Pearl necklace": How to avoid being busted by the Facebook cops of college sports. Retrieved from http://deadspin.com/5912230/dont-say-colt-45-or-pearl-necklace-how-to-avoid-being-busted-by-the-facebook-cops-of-college-sports

Dodds, P. (2012, July 31). Tom Daley Twitter controversy: UK police arrest teen over malicious tweets at Olympic diver. Retrieved from http://www.huffingtonpost.com/2012/07/31/tom-daley-twitter-police-olympic-diver_n_1722739.html

Entman, R. M. (1993). Framing: Toward clarification of a fractured paradigm. *Journal of Communication, 43,* 51–58.

ESPN.com news services. (2012, October 6). Cardale Jones: Classes pointless. *ESPN.* Retrieved October 6 from http://espn.go.com/collegefootball/story/_/id/8466428/ohio-state-buckeyes-cardale-jones-tweets-classes-pointless

Facebook. (2014). Company info. Retrieved from http://www.facebook.com/press/info.php?statistics

Florio, M. (2009, March 9). Eagles fire employee who complained about Dawkins' departure. Retrieved from http://profootballtalk.nbcsports.com/2009/03/09/eagles-fire-employee-who-complained-about-dawkins-departure/

Folger, J. (n.d.a). Implementing a small business social media strategy: Maintain your profiles. Retrieved from http://www.investopedia.com/university/implementing-small-business-social-media-strategy/maintain-your-profiles.asp

Folger, J. (n.d.b). Implementing a small business social media strategy: Build and develop your social media presence. Retrieved from http://www.investopedia.com/university/implementing-small-business-social-media-strategy/maintain-your-profiles.asp

Gibbs, A. (2015, February 2). Superbowl XLIX smashes Twitter records. Retrieved from http://www.cnbc.com/id/102388362

Gross, D. (2014, February 3). Super Bowl sets Twitter record. Retrieved from http://www.cnn.com/2014/02/03/tech/social-media/super-bowl-social-twitter

Hauer, M. (2013). The constitutionality of public university bans of student-athlete speech through social media. *Vermont Law Review, 37*, 413-436.

Huffington Post Sports. (2013, July 14). Roddy White reacts harshly to George Zimmerman verdict on Twitter. *Huffington Post.* Retrieved from http://www.huffingtonpost.com/2013/07/14/roddy-white-george-zimmerman-verdict-twitter_n_3593212.html

Jude, A. (2012, October 24). Oregon coach Chip Kelly says he trusts his players on Twitter. *The Oregonian.* Retrieved from http://www.oregonlive.com/ducks/index.ssf/2012/10/oregon_coach_chip_kelly_says_h_1.html

Kassing, J. W., & Sanderson, J. (2010). Tweeting through the Giro: A case study of fan-athlete interaction on Twitter. *International Journal of Sport Communication, 3*, 113–128.

Kuypers, J. A., & Cooper, S. D. (2005). A comparative framing analysis of embedded and behind-the-lines reporting on the 2003 Iraq War. *Qualitative Research Reports in Communication, 6*, 1–10.

Lepage, E. (n.d.). How to measure social media ROI for your business. Retrieved from http://blog.hootsuite.com/measure-social-media-roi-business/

LinkedIn's Newsroom. (n.d.). Retrieved from https://press.linkedin.com/

Love: McHale won't return. (2009, June 17). Retrieved from http://sports.espn.go.com/nba/news/story?id=4265512

MacMillan, D., & Rusli, E. M. (2014, August 26). Snapchat is said to have more than 100 million monthly active users. Retrieved from http://blogs.wsj.com/digits/2014/08/26/snapchat-said-to-have-more-than-100-million-monthly-active-users/

Matthews, C. (2014, January 15). More than 11 million young people have fled Facebook since 2011, according to one analyst estimate. Retrieved from http://business.time.com/2014/01/15/more-than-11-million-young-people-have-fled-facebook-since-2011/

McMenamin, D. (2012, May 18). Steve Blake, wife get hate tweets. Retrieved from http://espn.go.com/los-angeles/nba/story/_/id/7943732/steve-blake-los-angeles-lakers-wife-receive-threats-twitter

McMurphy, B. (2014, July 12). Bulldogs, Wildcats agree via Twitter. Retrieved from http://espn.go.com/college-football/story/_/id/11205943/mississippi-state-kansas-state-athletic-directors-agree-home-home-series-via-twitter

Meraz, S. (2009). Is there an elite hold? Traditional media to social media agenda setting influence in blogs networks. *Journal of Computer-Mediated Communication, 14*, 682–707.

Newell, S. (2014, August 10). Florida State's "Ask Jameis" hashtag was a predictable mess. Retrieved from http://deadspin.com/florida-states-ask-jameis-hashtag-was-a-predictable-m-1619082266

New Year's Eve programming and college football playoff seminfinals led Twitter. (2015, January 5). Retrieved from http://www.tvmediainsights.com/social-tv-buzz/new-years-eve-programming-college-football-playoff-semifinals-led-twitter/

Olson, E. (2013, October 29). Players can struggle when heckling turns to hate. Retrieved from http://sports.yahoo.com/news/players-struggle-heckling-turns-hate-190735810--ncaaf.html

Ortiz Jr., M. (2014, October 7). Ole Miss fans raise money to pay for fine and damages. Retrieved from http://dystnow.com/2014/10/07/ole-miss-fans-raise-money-to-pay-for-fine-and-damages/

Paxton, M. (2004). Gone fishin': A framing analysis of the fight over a small town's city seal. *Journal of Media and Religion, 3*, 43–55.

Present, B. (2013, April 8). No reasonable expectation of privacy on Facebook, judge says. Retrieved from http://www.thelegalintelligencer.com/id=1202532899353/No-Reasonable-Expectation-of-Privacy-on-Facebook-Judge-Says

Rashard Mendenhall doesn't hold back. (2011, May 4). Retrieved from http://sports.espn.go.com/Nfl/news/story?id=6471433

Recruit Yuri Wright expelled for tweets. (2012, January 20). Retrieved from http://espn.go.com/college-sports/recruiting/football/story/_/id/7484495/yuri-wright-twitter-posts-cost-college-scholarship

Safko, L., & Brake, D. K. (2009). *The social media Bible: Tactics, tools & strategies for business success.* Hoboken, New Jersey: John Wiley & Sons.

Sanderson, J. (2008). The Blog is Serving Its Purpose: Self-Presentation Strategies on. *Journal of Computer-Mediated Communication, 13*(4), 912–936. doi:10.1111/j.1083-6101.2008.00424.x

Sanderson, J. (2011a). *It's a whole new ballgame: How social media is changing sports.* New York, NY: Hampton Press.

Sanderson, J. (2011b). To tweet or not to tweet . . . : Exploring Division I athletic departments' social media policies. *International Journal of Sport Communication, 4*, 492–513.

Sanderson, J. (2013). Stepping into the (social media) game: Building athlete identity via Twitter. In R. Luppicini (Ed.), *Handbook of research on technoself: Identity in a technological society* (pp. 419–438). New York, NY: IGI Global.

Sanderson, J., & Browning, B. (2013). Training versus monitoring: A qualitative examination of athletic department practices regarding student-athletes and Twitter. *Qualitative Research Reports in Communication, 14,* 105–111.

Sanderson, J., Browning, B., & Schmittel, A. (2015). Education on the digital terrain: A case study exploring college athletes' perceptions of social media education. *International Journal of Sport Communication, 8,* 103–124.

Sanderson, J., & Emmons, B. (2014). Extending and withholding forgiveness to Josh Hamilton: Exploring forgiveness within parasocial interaction. *Communication and Sport, 2,* 24–47.

Sanderson J., & Kassing, J. W. (2014). New media and the evolution of fan-athlete interaction. In A. C. Billings & M. Hardin (Eds.), *The Routledge handbook of sport and new media* (pp. 247–270) New York, NY: Routledge.

Sanderson, J., & Truax, C. (2014). "I hate you man!": Exploring maladaptive parasocial interaction expressions to college athletes via Twitter. *Journal of Issues in Intercollegiate Athletics, 7,* 333–351.

Schwab, F. (2012, December 17). North Alabama player removed from team after racist tweet about Barack Obama. Retrieved from http://sports.yahoo.com/blogs/ncaaf-dr-saturday/north-alabama-player-removed-team-racist-tweet-barack-164244864--ncaaf.html

Smith, C. (2015, January 2). By the numbers: 45 amazing Google + statistics. Retrieved from http://expandedramblings.com/index.php/google-plus-statistics/2/

Tian, Y., & Stewart, C. M. (2005). Framing the SARS crisis: A computer-assisted text analysis of CNN and BBC online news reports of SARS. *Asian Journal of Communication, 15,* 289–301.

Tumblr. (n.d.). Retrieved from https://www.tumblr.com/about

Yoder, M. (2014, May 23). It was not a good idea for the Ravens to live tweet Ray Rice's press conference. Retrieved from http://www.sbnation.com/nfl/2014/5/23/5745888/ray-rice-wife-apology-assault-domestic-violence-ravens

Index

About the Authors

Jimmy Sanderson, PhD, earned a BA, MA, and PhD from Arizona State University in communication studies. He is currently an assistant professor in the Department of Communication Studies at Clemson University, where he directs the sports communication B.A. program. Prior to entering the academy, he worked in human resources management for 11 years. He maintains an active research agenda focused on the intersection of social media and sport, and also conducts research related to health and safety issues in sport. He has been cited in media outlets such as *USA Today*, *Chronicle of Higher Education*, and ESPN.com. He also regularly speaks to sport association groups about social media, such as the National Federation of State High School Associations and Academic Advisors for Athletics. He and his wife, Kirsten, have two boys, Walker and Connor. You can find him on Twitter: @jimmy_sanderson

Christopher Yandle was named assistant athletic director for communications & public relations at the Georgia Institute of Technology in July 2014 after two years in a similar role at the University of Miami. During his career, he assisted in the highly successful Robert Griffin III Heisman Trophy campaign in 2011, and was recognized as the 2014 CoSIDA Rising Star by his peers. A native of Houma, Louisiana, he attended the University of Southern Mississippi for two years before transferring to the University of Louisiana at Lafayette, where he graduated in 2004 with a BA in public relations. He received an MS in athletic administration from Marshall University in 2007. He and his wife, Ashleigh, have two kids, Addison and Jackson, and a French Bulldog named Tank. You can find him on Twitter: @chrisyandle